AYER Y AHORA

FoR DONNA –
WHO WILL SOON ADD HER
STORY TO THE AMERICAN
MOSAIC.

Robert Wolf
9-29-06

FREE RIVER PRESS FOLK LITERATURE SERIES

AYER Y AHORA
Yesterday and Today

Stories from Santa Fe
and
Northern New Mexico

Edited by
Robert Wolf

"Telling America's Story"

Free River Press
Lansning, Iowa

1. New Mexico   2. Hispanic culture   3. Folk Literature

FREE RIVER PRESS
Lansing, Iowa 52151

www.freeriverpress.org

CONTENTS

ACKNOWLEDGEMENTS

Thanks are due to the McCune Charitable Trust and the Santa Fe County and City Division of Senior Services for making this book possible. The McCune Charitable Trust funded the writing workshops which provided the bulk of the writings, and the Division of Senior Services provided workshop space in Santa Fe and Santa Cruz. Several of the Division's personnel, through their enthusiastic endorsement and hands-on involvement, provided invaluable help. Program Administrator Lupita Martinez publicized the workshops and helped in countless ways. Center Program Coordinator Carmen Chavez-Lujan made many necessary contacts and helped with the glossary. Program Secretary Gloria Polaco at the Mary Esther Gonzales Senior Center kept the list of sign-ups and, more important, did most of the work on the glossary. Carmen and Gloria also proofread the manuscript. Program Coordinator Cristina Villa helped organize the Santa Cruz workshop. Finally, I want to thank my long-time friend Tony Padilla for identifying the Mary Esther Gonzales Center as an ideal location for the workshop and for approaching Lupita Martinez with the idea of hosting it.

Preface

One is either drawn to the desert and to semi-arid lands, or one is repulsed. In the popular imagination New Mexico is associated with the desert, but in fact it is semi-arid. The landscape, for those of us who love it, is spectacular. It is a land of contrasts, of mountains and plains, canyons and mesas—hardly uniform in character. The state calls itself the Land of Enchantment, an apt label for a country noted for the clarity of its light, its epic cloud formations, the intensity of its sunsets.

The drama of the land has been matched for several centuries by the spirit, color, and beauty of its three contrasting cultures. To be sure, the edge has been taken off of each; but the homogenization that is concomitant with modernity has perhaps had less effect here than elsewhere in America. But loss there has been. And one of the purposes of this book is to record, implicitly and explicitly, cultural change in the eastern portion of northern New Mexico.

Up until fifty or sixty years ago, the native and Hispanic cultures retained much of the traditions and practices of their forebears. Aside from the Navajos, whose reservation extends from eastern Arizona into western New Mexico, the indigenous peoples of northern New Mexico are pueblo dwellers. "Anglo" is the term for the white population, but includes a mix of ethnic groups. Many if not most of Santa Fe's settlers in its early U.S. territorial years were Jewish merchants who brought goods to the city down the Santa Fe Trail from Kansas City. Many Hispanic families have Jewish blood and some Jewish settlers assimilated so completely into the Hispanic culture that over several centuries they lost most traces of Jewish culture and identity.

For over two centuries Santa Fe was the capital of the Spanish territory, New Mexico, which included what is now Texas, New Mexico, Arizona, California, Nevada, Utah, and Colorado. The first capital of New Mexico was San Gabriel, founded by Don Juan de Oñate in 1598. San Gabriel as capital was replaced by Santa Fe when it was founded in 1610. The Pueblo Revolt of

x AYER Y AHORA

1680 drove the Spanish from New Mexico, but the land was reconquered for Spain by Don Diego DeVargas in 1692, an event celebrated each September in Santa Fe with a three day fiesta.

Many years have passed since I experienced a Santa Fe fiesta. When I lived here from 1965 to 1974, fiesta was a wild time, with open houses going till early morning hours. Now, I imagine, parties are by invitation only and end at discrete times. In many other ways the atmosphere in Santa Fe began changing in 1974 when the city began to experience an influx of wealthy newcomers and change shifted into high gear. The new folks didn't come for the art. In fact, they may have known little or nothing of the nationally recognized artists who had been settling in Santa Fe and Taos for decades. Perhaps no one at that time suspected that the Canyon Road art colony and bohemian scene would soon vaporize, to be replaced by high rent art galleries that merchandized art by the square inch. Of the many artists I knew who lived on or near Canyon Road, not one lives in its vicinity today. As some of the stories in this anthology indicate, Santa Fe has lost most of its characters; those who are left have mellowed with age. The cultural shift on Canyon Road is emblematic of the shift throughout the city.

The original impulse that led to the book was my desire to document the Canyon Road scene in the sixties and seventies through the reminiscences of those artists still in town. But fortunately that vision expanded to one that entailed documenting more comprehensive change. The McCune Charitable Foundation was sympathetic with that goal and provided project funding while the Santa Fe County and City Division of Senior Services donated the workshop space. A group of approximately fourteen seniors met for five consecutive days in early January 2006 at the Mary Esther Gonzales Senior Center in Santa Fe. Three of the same group met with seven other seniors in the Santa Cruz senior center, which is also administered by the Division of Senior Services, for three days in February. And finally, most of the Santa Fe group plus four new writers met again at the Mary Esther Gonzales Senior Center for a final three days in March. This book is a selection from the writings produced at those workshops, along with three stories that were written in workshop I conducted in Santa Fe in 1998.

In the January workshop I asked the Hispanic members, almost all of whom had grown up in northern villages, for stories that would illustrate village life in those days. I asked for process stories, descriptions of how certain things were done, and for activities that have disappeared. The anglos, on the other hand, wrote on a variety of topics that would give people who have never been to New Mexico a feel for characters and places now and then. One example is the poem by Denise Lynch, based on a story she wrote in the workshop, which evokes memories of a childhood in the Canyon Road neighborhood. Only one writer in that workshop was not from New Mexico, and she wrote a story that included a description of sorghum making in Alabama. It is, by implication, a good companion piece for the Hispanic process stories.

In the Santa Cruz workshop I asked the participants, "What has been the most significant cultural loss for Hispanics?" Without hesitating, several members answered, "The loss of Spanish." People instinctively recognize that once their language is lost, the rest of their culture goes with it. That is why the Pueblo of Pojoaque, which is rebuilding its Tewa culture, is now hiring only Tewa speaking teachers for its school. Similarly, in western New Mexico the Hopi are teaching their language to young tribal members because for years younger people could not speak it.

Something faintly analogous to that is happening to the American language. Our working, everyday vocabularies are shrinking. So are our writers' vocabularies, perhaps in response to what most readers can understand without reaching for a dictionary. The latest infusion of energy into the American language has come from black Americans. Without them, our language and indeed our culture would be severely impoverished. Yet we need more infusions of energy, and so I encouraged the workshop writers to use Spanish words whenever they felt the need or whim. Those words that are not explained in the text are defined in a glossary at the end.

Most of us feel great loss at the disappearance of one cultural tradition after another. The impersonal techniques that continue to supercede handicrafts and low tech know-how seem destined to obliterate the human presence from every phase of work. But that needn't be the case. When we look about us we see examples of people working to create communities with human centered economies and cultures. But that work is being done by those already committed to community. And writing workshops and community study circles are not a bad way to begin the community building process. The Santa Fe writing workshops had the festive nature of a reunion, for while most of us had not known each other in years past, we had frequented the same places and observed the same characters. Common experiences began pulling us closer as a group. The experience has been exhilarating for all of us.

AURORA G. SALAZAR

Aurora G. Salazar was born and raised in Wagon Mound, New Mexico. She was married to Max J. Salazar. They had four children, Connie and Yolanda, and two that died in infancy, Eugene and Wilma. She taught school in Wagon Mound for seventeen-and-a-half years. The family moved to Santa Fe where Aurora taught for fifteen years. Since her retirement she has been active in several organizations and does volunteer work for a number of community programs.

LA SEMANA SANTA

My parents and grandparents owned a large ranch which they had homesteaded, about eighteen miles from Wagon Mound, a small community in northeastern Mora County. We spent most of the time there.

My grandfather was a member of the *Hermanos de Jesus Cristo*, the Brothers of Jesus Christ, a large fraternal Catholic men's organization that had its roots in Spain. The *morada* was on his property. It was a one room adobe structure nestled close to the ground on the grassy hillside.

The *Semana Santa* rituals and ceremonies that took place at that time are among the happiest and most vivid memories of my earliest childhood.

In the context of the times, and because of geographical isolation, the *hermandad* fulfilled the spiritual, worldly, and even the judicial needs of the people. They adhered to a very rigid code of ethics based on Christian principles. Because their rules were so strict and harsh, my grandfather would not allow his son, my uncle, to become a member.

Semana Santa was the last week of Lent. It was totally dedicated to spiritual services. The preparations for this holy time were made many days beforehand. The local ranch hands and the men in the family cleaned the grounds, out-buildings and all the surrounding area. All the *hermanos* and their families from the nearby ranches came to congregate and worship at the *morada*. They all stayed at the ranch. There were horses to be fed and watered, as well as people to be lodged and nourished. They chopped huge, monstrous piles of firewood to be used for heating and cooking. No heavy manual labor or extraneous activities were permitted during the holy days—Wednesday, Thursday and Friday—before Easter. There would be no music, singing or dancing.

My mother and her cousins would construct an altar in the corner of the long, wide dining room. It had been stripped of all furniture except chairs and *tarimas* that were placed around the room. The altar walls and the altar were covered with pristine white cloths. A large primitive, hand carved crucifix was hung on one side and framed pictures of saints were placed on the other.

Tall, dark wooden candleholders were placed on the altar. The perimeter of the area was decorated with colorful crepe paper flowers that we had made. At the end of the celebration they were carefully stored, to be used again from year to year.

The women would prepare huge quantities of food—*posole*, *chicos*, beans, dried *quelites*, and *rueditas*. It was a time of abstinence, no meat. They baked dozens of beautiful golden loaves of bread, fragrant spicy pies made of dried apples, apricots, peaches and prunes, as well as huge mounds of delicious anise flavored *biscochitos* baked in the *horno*, the outdoor adobe oven.

One by one the horse drawn wagons and buggies arrived. There were people of all ages, old people, young children and even infants. They were laden with clothes, bedding, "goodies," and provisions. How excited and happy we all were! There were hugs and kisses and joyful words of welcome. My sister and I were so happy and eager to have the younger children because we rarely had playmates.

When all had finally arrived and got settled, the men retreated to the morada for the duration of the celebration. The women and children remained in the house to do the cooking and cleaning, and to prepare the house for the *visitas* and *velorios* that were held nightly. Food was prepared and sent to the men at the *morada* for each meal.

We children were given daily chores. We brought in the wood, water from the well, fed the chickens and gathered the eggs. It was such fun to go into the chicken coop, barns and the hayloft. We laughed and shouted, "Look how many I found!" when we had found a nest. We were assigned to the large attic room above the first story main rooms. It was now covered with wall to wall mattresses, bed rolls and warm, cozy blankets. What fun we had, being careful to stifle our laughter, for we had to be quiet. We built tents, turned somersaults on the cushy floor, played "statue" and other games.

Once a day the hermanos came to pray at the altar. At home, we watched for the procession as they came from the morada. They came slowly across the rough, barren ground. At times, one or two brothers would carry a large, heavy wooden *madero* made of thick logs. On occasion, they were accompanied by a few flagellants—men with black shrouds that covered their heads, and stripped to the waist, flogging themselves with long *disciplinas* made of rope. They walked slowly to the rhythm of the whips, with the red blood streaming down their backs. They entered the room and shut the door to conduct their own private rituals. We children would stealthily creep up the stairs to the attic room. Being curious and inquisitive, as children are, we would softly creep to our "secret" viewing place—a small knot hole on the floor, which was the ceiling of the altar room. We would take turns viewing the scene below. I shudder to think what horrendous punishment would have been meted to us if we had been discovered.

The hermanos were strict disciplinarians. Woe unto anyone who had to answer for his misdeeds. At one time my young uncle and his cousin were sent to deliver a large wooden trunk-like chest from the house to the morada. Boys being boys, they thought they would play a joke on them. There were some skeleton remains of animals here and there on the pasture land. They gathered them and put them inside the chest and slowly trekked their way to the morada, carrying the heavy chest. They knocked on the door, left the chest, and ran all the way home, laughing and chuckling, as they imagined how horrified the brothers would be when they opened the door. But their glee was short-lived. The very next day my grandfather sent word to my grandmother to send the boys to the morada. The two culprits went, dragging their feet. They presented themselves, quaking with fear, dreading the punishment they would get. They tearfully confessed and asked to be forgiven. For their penance they were given a large pail. They were ordered to fill it with the gravely sand from the ant hills that were in the area. Then they had to make two crosses on the ground with the gravel. They had to roll up their pants' legs, bare their knees, kneel on the rough sand, and stretch out their arms. A heavy rock was placed on each hand. They knelt, painfully shifting from one knee to the other, tears streaming down their faces. After a while they were released and sent home and admonished to behave themselves.

Sometimes we could see from our house, across the *acequia*, a penitente on the rocky hillside slowly walking back and forth, flagellating himself. It was said that some did it as a sacrifice, as a prayer, in atonement, or in punishment.

There would be *velorios* at the house in the evenings. These were held to pray devoutly. They would also sing *alabados*, mournful hymns of the Passion. The *Rezador* would lead the congregation in prayer. Sometimes my grandfather, who was proud that I could read Spanish, would have me read aloud some of the prayers. I must have been about seven years old; I felt so proud and important!

On Good Friday afternoon we would all go to pray the Stations of the Cross. They had been laid out on the ground near the morada, each station marked with a short wooden cross.

A penitente carried a heavy cross on his back. Some of them, with shrouded heads, stripped to the waist, whipped themselves, first across one shoulder and then the other, as they walked along. Once, I loudly asked my grandmother, "Who washes their bloody whips and clothes?" She promptly pinched my arm and hushed me.

That night there would be a velorio and *tinieblas*, the Tenebrae. It was a solemn somber service simulating the darkness, the quaking of the earth and the thunderous tumult that occurred when Christ died. All the lamps and candles were extinguished. Then the brothers chanted prayers moaningly, the *matracas* were whirled, making their clackety noises. Large, heavy metal chains were pounded and thumped noisily on the floor, again and again; the chanting and moaning went on and on. Children were not allowed to attend this ceremony, for it was too eerie and frightening.

The next day everyone packed their belongings, harnessed their horses, and loaded their wagons. There were a lot of heartfelt and tearful good-byes. We all hugged and waved saying, *"Adios," "Vuelvan pronto," "Vayan con Dios,"*—"Goodbye," "Come back soon," "May God go with you." My sister and I were sad, we would miss our friends and the good times we had enjoyed. My folks, I'm sure, would breathe sighs of relief, as they went back to work and got things back to normal.

SOPHIA JARAMILLO

Sophia Jaramillo was born in December 1921 in the small mining town of Dawson, New Mexico. At age five or six her family moved to a large cattle ranch in Cimarron, New Mexico, the source of many of her family stories. Sophia, a writer, self-published her first book, Once Upon A time . . . . A Gathering of Writings. *One of her stories has appeared in* La Herencia, *a local publication. She is now working on a second gathering of stories of local people and is about half finished with her first novel,* Suenos del Norte, *a story of an orphan who becomes "El Patron Grande" del Norte.*

POLITICS AT THE CORRAL

"Baaa, baaa!" This was the sound of a calf lassoed and brought to the ground and readied for branding! The next sound was that of

a sizzling hot iron on its raw hide . . . and the whistling and yelling from the cowboys roosting at the top of the corral fence. A
calf was brought up and the WS brand was distinctly imprinted
on its left quadrant. Two expert hands made the calf into a steer
with a simple operation, rocky mountain oysters were collected
for dinner, and the steer was set free in the corral to suffer its
indignities.

This was branding time at the WS, an event where neighbor-
ing cowboys were invited to come give a hand. My father was
manager, and he had invited cowboy friends from Raton, Las
Vegas, Taos, Maxwell and Springer. They arrived before six that
morning, dressed for work and ready to raise a little hell. They
took turns roping, branding, and performing the operation.

While some worked, others took time to roost at the top of
the corral fence and whoop it up. They whistled, laughed and
hollered, and made obnoxious statements. Cowboys are a kind
all their own.

In between brandings the roosters at the top of the corral fence
made their way to the north end, where they formed a small circle
and each brought out his own brand of whiskey, a bottle of Wild
Turkey, Johnny Walker or whatever, and passed it around. This
started another round of laughter, back slapping, whistling and
wild noises. From where I sat on the bed of an empty wagon, all
I could see in the circle were six or seven ten-gallon hats, worn
out Levis, and dirty messed up boots. They moved about like wild
men. What I saw this day made me promise myself never to marry
a cowboy.

I was about nine years old and had been given permission to
stay home with my mother, and together we watched the branding. This was my first time, and would be my last! My mother
and I slid our heads outside the lower boards of the corral, and for
the most part watched from a distance.

"This is man's work and it must be done," Mama said.

"Mama, why did you give me permission to come to this horrible event?"

"I could not have stopped you if I hadn't," she said.

Branding time on the WS Ranch was as exciting as a Fourth of July rodeo. This particular day was not too accommodating for the cowboys wearing three-inch heels: it had intermittently rained and shined, and when the rain came, it played havoc in the corral grounds, creating a shitty mess with the mixture of rain and cow chips. However, this was a special occasion, and it was important that each cowboy have an hour of fame with a performance.

Sometime in the middle of the morning, when the rain had subsided, we saw a long black car slither into the driveway. As a man stepped out of the car, we could tell he was not dressed for the ranch. He wore a navy blue pin-striped suit, a fancy white shirt with cuff links and a red tie. He wore fancy leather shoes and a small hat; someone said it was a derby.

Another person sitting at the top of the corral fence said it was our senator, a Democrat, who was running for re-election. With an aggressive gait he came to the corral and introduced himself proudly: "I am your United States senator from New Mexico," and then asked who was the ranch manager. He was told it was Sandy, who was inside branding calves, and that he might have to wait a little while. Someone offered him a place to sit on top of the fence. Two of the cowboys lifted him up so he would not get his shoes in the unga.

The senator made himself at home, and at times hollered with the wild cowboys when another calf had been branded. My father, learning that a man was looking for him, came out from his post and greeted the visitor. I doubt very much if he knew who it was. You see, my father was a dyed-in-the-wool Republican, and did not give a damn who the man was.

The senator came down from the fence, offered his hand and introduced himself. "I was just going by for a rally to Raton, and I saw all the activity here among your cowboys. I wonder if you will allow me a little time to address them. I am running for re-election, and I need every vote I can get."

My father was kind and gracious. "Senator, we've got important work to do, and very little time for politics. So get started."

"Thank you. I will make it in a hurry."

The Senator having moved back to his perch at the top of the corral, expounded on his virtues in Washington, D.C. and promised that if he were re-elected, he would see to it that New Mexico received all the water it needed and sufficient rangeland to make ours the most lucrative ranch in the whole country.

There was a lot of clapping and whistling for the senator, but from somewhere in the corral, someone yelled, "Unga!"

The Senator was not particularly perturbed.

My father thanked him for taking time to talk with "his boys" and explained that not too many politicians stopped by. He invited him to stay for the remainder of the branding and to come later in the evening to have some rocky mountain oysters for dinner.

The senator looked at his watch and said he must leave but hoped to see them later that evening for the Rocky Mountain celebration!

Two of the cowboys helped him down from the fence, reminding him not to step on the unga.

As the Senator drove away from the ranch, he may have seen a sign on the road: *"You are now leaving Cimarron, where pavement ends and hell begins."*

P.S. I did not marry a cowboy!

MERCEDES ROYBAL

Mercedes Roybal lives in Santa Fe with her husband. They have five children and nine grandchildren. She was born and raised in Pecos, New Mexico. She is a retired school teacher who loves to travel, loves life, and loves to write.

THE SATURDAY NIGHT DANCE

The big shindig that we all enjoyed was the Saturday night dance, either at Glorieta or Pecos. Besides these dances, others were held to celebrate feast days, weddings, fiestas, and other special occasions. For wedding dances the musicians played all afternoon and way into the night. Everybody danced; yes, everybody danced. I always felt such happiness when I knew that there would be a dance. It was a special celebration. I remember praying to St. Anthony of Padua (patron saint of lost items) asking him to help me find a wonderful dancing partner. Not just an ordinary dancing partner, but a good looking one.

I felt that it was absolutely necessary to dance all night. The dance was where all the action was, it was where you saw all your friends and cousins and the place to wear your new outfit or your new shoes. The community dance was a super special social.

Early Saturday we did any necessary work, such as cleaning and baking. We behaved like angels because we needed to be on good terms with Mom and Dad. First you did all your work and then you got ready. You curled your hair and next you had to convince your parents that it was terribly important for you to attend. The whole world was going to be there.

Your parents had to take you because you were not allowed to go alone. However, they might let you go with some responsible adult, like a cousin or a neighbor. If your parents were upset with you, they would not allow you to go to the dance. That was real punishment, that hurt.

About a hundred or more attended the dances. These included adults, who also enjoyed dancing but didn't relish it like we did. The whole family attended wedding dances. Some couples even took their young baby in a small basket and shoved the basket with the sleeping child under the bench while they enjoyed a dance. The adults would entertain us with some old fashioned dances like the *el valse, las cuadrillas or el baile del pano* and many more. It was entertaining and absolutely great.

The custom of the regular dance was for young girls to sit in a half circle around the dance floor and for the boys or young men to stand in a space behind them. When the music started the young men would come and ask the girls to dance.

The women could not or should not refuse the request. It was considered very bad manners. That was called *"el desigre,"* or the refusal, and you just didn't do that. During intermission several friendly dance hall personnel would come around and collect the ten cent fee from the male partner. That interval provided you with enough time to chat or flirt with your partner.

You might even check out who was wearing what and who had been lucky enough to be asked to dance. If you weren't asked out to dance you sat there and pretended that you didn't care. The idea was to get the attention of some young man so that he would notice you and ask you to dance the next time. If you were popular, you would dance all night and that was terrific. I must have been popular because I remember dancing all night and I loved that.

On Monday morning when we went back to school, that's all you talked about and boy did we exaggerate about how we had danced all night. *"Algunas pobres solamente habian bailado los ojos."* Some poor souls had only danced their eyes.

"Hay Chihuahua!" Those were memorable good old days!

MERCEDES ROYBAL

THE LITTLE GOAT GIRL

I was born in a quiet, picturesque community right outside of Pecos. My parents were humble farmers who owned sheep, goats, chickens, horses and a few cattle. I never considered our family poor. I thought we were regular people, proud of our heritage and culture. I remember Mom and Dad telling us how important it was to never depend on welfare. They wanted us to be honest about our language and our roots, and proud of our humble beginnings. Telling this story is perhaps a way to comply with their wishes. I'm the Little Goat Girl from Pecos, and I'm proud of it. It was an honest living and a grand childhood.

Perhaps I was a little haughty, at least that is how I remember those days. My many feisty cousins lived all around us and I don't remember any of them having to take care of goats. We were a proud bunch.

My husband tells me that he thought I was a snob. He said he was afraid to talk to me. I was from west Pecos and he was from east Pecos, on the other side of the river. The west Pecos kids considered the east Pecos kids to be from Timbuktoo. I felt he was a *morodo*. He tells me I was a know-it-all.

My parents had to work hard and they did have hired help to assist with the sheep and other large animals. We kept a few goats close to home for the milk, cheese and the *cabritos* that when butchered and roasted were very tasty. I thought goats were for poor, needy people, but we were not needy or poor, yet my parents insisted on keeping these stinky goats. Yet these frisky, smelly goats were special. They were like pets and we even had special names for them. I was the lucky, or at times unlucky, one who had to look after then in the summer, on weekends, and, during the school year, after classes. I was the designated goat girl.

I would take the small group of goats and their babies out to pasture; it was a necessary chore, but in certain ways a pleasure. I was supposed to take them out to the nearby fields and forest and it was not a big deal for me, if I could just keep it a secret.

I was like some of the characters in the children's stories I loved to read, about girls like Heidi who took care of goats. I loved these animals, and I loved the long leisurely walks. I thought I was blessed and thinking back, I was. Then why did I insist on keeping it a secret? Because goats don't have the prestige that cattle do and this proud young girl didn't want to be teased. In elementary school boys love to tease and tease me they would. I can still hear the Ortiz boys from Pecos and the Ruiz boys from Rowe chasing me and pulling my braids and calling me *cabrera*, or little goat girl. I look back now and I think surely they had a crush on me that that was their way of showing it.

I can still hear my parents' voices: "Goats are good, goats are necessary, and we need them."

LYDIA LOPEZ

Lydia Lopez, wife and mother of seven, grandmother of twelve, great-grandmother of two, served as a substitute teacher in her spare time. Twelve generations of her family were raised in the beautiful Española Valley of northern New Mexico — her grandfather was a trustee of the Santa Cruz land grant, her great-grandfather went on the Santa Fe Trail to bring supplies to the colonists before the railroad came to this region. Lydia has always been a writer; these writing workshops have served as an opportunity to write her childhood memories for her children and grandchildren so that they will know their roots.

EL MOLINO DE JUAN (JOHN'S FLOUR MILL)

This crisp October morning Juan rose quickly, putting on his favorite *pecheras*, grabbing a quick breakfast of scrambled eggs wrapped in a warm tortilla prepared by Lucia, his young wife, who had risen early to prepare this hearty meal! Off he rushed to begin his daily routine of checking his monstrous engine, filling first the tank with gasoline, then filling the water tank that would cool the huge motor, checking the belts, and finally cranking the machine to life. The noisy contraption came alive!

The whole village was awakened by the deafening sound. Everyone in Santo Niño heard the noise. Juan's *molino* was bustling with frantic activity as he went about the business of checking the grinding stones and the sifters that separated the crushed grains into flour and bran, filtering them into aluminum tubs holding the flour, switching the full ones and setting the empty ones in place, filling the chute with grain again and again. Running, changing, filling, emptying, people waiting, people bringing sacks of wheat to be ground, unloading, loading, Juan looking more and more like a white ghost, even his eyelashes covered by the flour dust that rose up throughout the mill!

Juanito, his eldest son, would help customers with the orders of wheat to be ground. They arrived in wagons pulled by teams of horses, some coming from as far as Truchas in the high mountains twelve or more miles away! They came prepared to spend the night, sleeping under their wagons, feeding and watering their horses, tending to a common fire where they warmed their meals. Juan worked tediously without stopping, the engine chugging away furiously, crushing and sifting endlessly!

At lunchtime Lucia would send her eight-year-old daughter, Eloise, with a lard bucket full of tortillas, folded and filled with meat and *chili verde*, a large jar of cold water for thirsty Juan and Juanito, which was consumed in no time! The engine working through the night, lit by a single battery lamp! Juan would hand Eloise a bucket to fetch water from a well in the center of the hacienda-shaped compound. Eloise slowly lowered the bucket into the deep well, let it fill with water, poured the water into her father's bucket, proceeded to the mill, and with each heavy step tried not to spill a precious drop. Eloise handed the bucket to her father to feed the thirsty tank that cooled the huge engine. The noise was deafening, but the bucket handed back to Eloise had a silent message: "Bring me some more water, *mi hita!*"

The earth shattering noise awoke the cows, pigs, and chickens as well. Lucia's Holstein cow, Bossy, had been milked and turned into the grazing pasture to eat the last green blades of grass that fall morning. But Bossy smelled a familiar smell in the air, so she followed the scent of sweet bran fed to her the previous day and broke through the fence, headed in the direction of the flour mill. Juan readied a large wooden box, filled with bran for Bossy. After having her fill, Juan tied a rope around her neck, handed it to the water bearer/lunch carrier/now cow shepherd . . . me, Eloise!

AVA LEE HOLLY

Ava Lee Holly was born in Alabama where she attended school for the blind. From the fourth grade until she married, Ava Lee taught braille and for six years worked for the Florida Council for the Blind. Ava Lee has three daughters. She moved to Santa

Fe in 2002.

MAKING SORGHUM SYRUP

Just before spring began to bud farmers would be talking about breaking ground. That is when they would plow the ground and plan their planting. Some years the ground would be too wet to plow and they would have to wait until it was drier. Sometimes they were late in planting. I remember they liked to plant corn March 17, so there would be 180 frost free days for corn to grow. My brother, Newburn, and I would help by carrying fertilizer or seed from where it was at the end of rows to where Daddy needed it. Summertime there was always hoeing and weeding and, as the fruit and vegetables matured, there was canning and drying fruits and vegetables for the coming winter.

In the early fall, my favorite time of year, the sorghum cane was ripe and ready for making syrup. Picking cotton was hard work but making sorghum syrup was a lot of fun for children. We would strip the fodder off the cane, which I liked to do but sometimes I would tangle up with a wasp or two. That was no fun. After the fodder was stripped off, the cane was cut; then the seed heads had to be cut off.

Early the next morning Daddy would take his load of cane to the mill. He would hitch up a team of horses to a large pole and get his cane crushed so there would be juice to start the making of syrup. Every load that came after his was first come, first served. All day cane was crushed, juice was strained and then poured into the large pan where it was boiled in about ten stages until it was as thick as each farmer wanted it. Daddy liked his syrup heavy, thick. Of course the thicker the syrup the sooner it would turn to sugar. By the sugar getting thick meant that we would have to re-heat it as we ate it. It sure was good with hot biscuits.

Mama would stay home and prepare a big picnic lunch. There would be other families at the mill with their lunch so it would be a good neighborhood gathering, not only to share a picnic but also to share work.

About one o'clock Mama would tell Newburn and me that we could go on to the syrup mill. We took off and did not play around getting there. We knew there would be some fun things and some work as soon as we arrived. Someone would give us a bowl of skimmings which formed on the syrup when it was in a fast boil. One thing we had to watch out for was yellow jackets. They liked cane juice and skimmings too.

Before we arrived at the mill we heard Mr. Fault, our neighbor, cursing. We knew who he was and we were afraid of him. He cursed so much we could tell that he was very angry. As soon as we saw him we began to run. About half of his cane had slipped off the back end of his wagon. He was just standing there, looking at it and cursing. If it had been any one of our neighbors but him we would have asked for a stalk of cane. We did not need a stalk of cane as there would be plenty of juice and skimmings for us. As soon as we told Daddy what had happened he sure had a good laugh, which was good for him because he had been working hard for several hours.

This was during the Depression and farmers helped each other. These farms were small and I doubt if any small farmers are raising cane today like they did then because it would be too labor intensive. I think that neighbors today are too busy to help each other.

LYDIA LOPEZ

RISTRAS

As a young girl I lived in the small village of Santo Niño, near Santa Cruz de la Cañada, the village where the Spanish colonists settled after the Pueblo Revolt of 1680. Families lived close to each other and helped each other—making *matanzas*, building with adobes, plastering with mud, making coffins, lending a hand in any emergency.

Everyone in my village spoke Spanish. My first language was Spanish. My parents farmed about ten acres and grew an enormous garden. They grew *chili* and corn (sweet, blue, and white), peas, green beans, *calabacitas*, juicy cantaloupes, huge watermelons, peaches (my favorite fruit), apples (Red Delicious), cherries, apricots and nice plump plums.

When harvest time came, my older sisters and I would help our mother pick bushel after bushel of ripe red chili pods and haul each bushel to a trailer my father had made for this purpose. He would hitch it up to the tractor and let me drive it ever so slowly to our house a short distance away. My two older sisters, being stronger than I, would carry the colorful bushels of chiles into one of our bedrooms, which had been emptied of furniture.

The chile picking had to be done either before going to school, bright and early, or after school, as our parents made our education a priority. On weekends our cousins would come to help, as chile does not ripen all at once. Thank goodness!

Lucia, my mother, was in charge of making the beautiful fragrant *ristras*. It was a tedious job. She first sorted the red chiles by size—the nicest in one pile, the crooked in another pile, the orange colored not-quite-ripe in another.

Mother would send me to our neighbor Magdalena's home to ask her to come and help with the rest of ristra making. Magdalena was a strong but gentle woman in her late forties with milk white skin and dark curly hair, who had been crippled either by birth or through some accident.

Mother and Magdalena would first tie three chiles together with string and take three more and tie them to the same string, and three more, until they had a three or four foot string of chiles. Mother would measure her height with a length of heavy twine and start weaving the chile strings around the twine. The ristra tying would last until midnight. When my sisters and I awoke the next morning, the room would be filled with all the ristras lying lengthwise on the floor! They were ready to be hung up by my father, as they were heavy. He climbed the ladder and hung each ristra outside on a *viga* to dry in the warm sun. After all these trips up the ladder with ristras, he must have been as tired as Mother.

What a colorful sight greeted us when we returned from school! The outside walls of our house had turned bright rich red. All that hard work so we could enjoy the savory, fragrant, hot red chile our mother would fix for us with warm soft *tortillas,* or in a steaming bowl of *posole.*

Magdalena would return to help us set our room back in order and Mother would pay her and send her home with her arms full of whatever we had to share.

PATRICIA D'ANDREA

Pat D'Andrea grew up in New Mexico and has lived in Santa Fe since the 1970s.

TAMALES

Santa Fe is the "City Different." That means that the whole city is supposed to look like it's made of adobe, whether it is or not.

There are neighborhoods here which are more than a hundred years old and not made of adobe. One of these is a small neighborhood one block south of the capitol that was built when the railroad almost got to town in the 1860s. It's one short street called East Santa Fe Avenue. Most of the houses are brick bungalow style with pitched roofs, porches and small fenced yards. There are big elm trees along both sides of this street and the sidewalks have all buckled because the tree roots have pushed them up at the seams. Little skateboard ramps—up and down. It was hard to walk on those sidewalks in 1973 when I lived there.

That year Sofía, the Escamilla's daughter from next door, had moved back to town from Mexico City with her husband and their three boys. He was a professional wrestler, a real one, not a showy TV wrestler who wears silver capes. There wasn't any work for him in Santa Fe. So they decided to cook for a living. Sofía was a wonderful cook. I guess she said, "Why not?"

One Christmas, Sofía, Antonio and their boys decided to make *tamales* for the Christmas trade. The boys were little, rambunctious, and not useful in the kitchen. That left Antonio, also not useful, Sofia's parents (too old), and, finally, Sofía.

She had started by making *biscochitos*, which were very popular with the neighbors. Tamales were more difficult, complicated and demanding, but Sofía was determined. Would I help? she asked. Sure, I said. Little did I know.

Sofía got together a team—Olivama (short, stout, and quiet) came from up north in Peñasco. Julia and Rosalinda, dyed-blonde sisters from Delicias in Chihuahua, sang a lot and worked so fast no one else could keep up. The big work began on December 23, a Tuesday, but before that Sofía had boiled the chicken and pork, shredded the meats and mixed them with Chimayo red *chile* powder, garlic, oil, *comino*, salt and pepper.

Olivama mixed the *masa* with the broth, chile and comino and kept the big table supplied with huge bowls of the dough. She was also responsible for soaking the *hojas* in the sink until they were soft, then spreading them on a towel at the big table.

Julia and Rosalinda smoothed the masa on the corn husks with spatulas, then laid them on the table next to me. I put a tablespoon of meat on each. Sofia folded and wrapped the tamales, stacked them in the big steamers on the stove, and set them to cook. When the tamales were cooked and then cooled, Olivama wrapped them in waxed paper, Sofía put them in plastic bags, one dozen in each, and then into the big refrigerator.

The dark kitchen seemed brighter in the heat from the stove, full of the smell of good red chile, garlic, comino and anise. The little boys ran in and out, Julia and Rosalinda sang, Olivama worked quietly, Sofía was everywhere, full of energy, her dark hair standing out like it was electrified. When we stopped for *empanadas* and coffee, Sofía told us, "We've got to make eighty dozen by tomorrow." By seven we'd made twenty dozen. Long night ahead.

Not being a cook myself, I'd offered to do this work in exchange for a "lifetime supply" of tamales, *biscochitos*, and *empanadas.* Also, I had the idea that being a neighbor meant helping out, something I'd already learned from our small street.

About eleven thirty Antonio came in with a bottle of José Cuervo Especial and a bottle of Rom Pope.

"Remember," he said, "José Cuervo does not do time."

That started Julia and Rosalinda on a round of jokes and toasts. *"Viva Méjico!" "Viva tamale!"* and so on. The *tequila* was sharp, the Rom Pope was smooth and sweet.

Pretty soon I had a little bit more and we sang a version of *La Cucaracha.* By this time, even Olivama was singing. We toasted each other again.

After a while, Sofía said, "Time to go home," and I remember her guiding me to the door and me stumbling down the steps, through the gate and into my own back yard, breathing in the cold air and the smell of red chile on my hands.

Sometime the next morning, seemed like it was really early but maybe not, I heard the front door bell. It was Sofía.

She looked at me closely and said, "Could you do a little more?"

"Sure," I said.

By then they were on dozen number sixty-three and they were all tired, so I took over one job after another while each one rested. And I ate a lot of tamales, the ones that weren't perfect. By that afternoon when we finished I had probably eaten two dozen tamales.

After all the tamales were delivered that Christmas Eve, the kitchen seemed too quiet. We all had bowls of posole, Noche Buena beer and laughed about the two dozen tamales I'd eaten. Then we hugged each other and went out into the snow to go home.

MARGARET RICE-JETTE

Margaret Rice-Jette is a painter who is inspired by the enchanted landscapes and skyscapes of northern New Mexico. Originally

*from Baltimore, she has lived in Santa Fe County since 1971,
amid the rich diversity of native American, Hispanic and anglo
cultures. She has an MFA in painting and has been artist in resi-
dence at Mercy University in Macon, Georgia, has taught locally
in private schools, and held workshops for teens and adults. Her
three sons reside in Santa Fe and she has three granddaughters.*

THE SMALL THEFT

It was a drought year in all of New Mexico. In Pojoaque that
summer the fields were so dry that walking through them raised
clouds of yellow dust. Hordes of grasshoppers rose in front of me
as I hauled pails of water to corn already stunted.

One morning Pablita came over with serious advice on the
practical way to steal water from the *Acequia Baranca.*

"You only open the gate a little. Prop it with a stick, a small
one, you understand, so it looks natural. If you do it right it won't
be noticed. Besides, your garden needs to survive. A bad year."

Since there are famous El Rancho stories of people being shot
for just such a small invasion of water rights, I listened but was
not tempted.

A few weeks later I witnessed Pablita's monumental anger.
She had been caught at it. She, Pablita, wife of the *majordomo*!
The indignity of the fine was one thing, but the laughter of her
neighbors and all her many relations who enjoyed a good joke
was hard to take.

All day her face burned from keeping her own tongue in check.
Adolpho's added teasing, no matter how sweetly sly, stung more
than mortal woman should be expected to endure.

She had delayed facing her husband by inviting me over for
coffee.

Adolpho spoke to me, but the content was for Pablita. "You
see, Margarita, it doesn't pay to steal. Look, we will have a good
rain soon. God provides."

Pablita slammed out of the house. The screen door jumped
on its hinges.

"The good God provides," she said. "Yes, if I help!" She threw a lethal look back at Adolpho through the screen and then turned to me. "Margarita, don't listen. This is the first time I've been caught in many years, not so bad, you see!"

Adolpho came slowly out of the house and looked innocently up at the sky as if he could see high clouds piled up over the mountains. Wisps there each afternoon only to drift away from the valley.

"It will rain tonight."

"Adolpho, you grow old. Now your bones tell the weather. If it rains, it will rain in the mountains, not here."

The air crackled around Pablita. She carried her personal storm out to the garden to hoe away her frustration.

That night wind carried the storm clouds into the valley. It began to rain. It rained all the next day.

On the following day when I woke up and found it was still raining, I put on old clothes and a slicker, took a shovel, and went to my garden before breakfast. Across the fields I saw my neighbors marching like a silent army to their gardens, shovel weapons over their shoulders. My collies were having a good time getting in my way as I dug little trenches to drain the deluge from new plants.

Across the lower alfalfa fields I saw Adolpho helping Pablita save her tomato plants. He bent to speak to her. Maybe he whispered, "God will provide."

MARGARET RICE-JETTE

CULTURAL EXCHANGE

Pablita is excited about redoing her *casita* in wall-to-wall plastic.

"Those new trailers—t hey're beautiful! So easy to keep up. I looked at Eloy's and decided to do over this old house modern."

She has invited me over to share her enthusiasm for progressive change. I look. Try to think of something to say. She bubbles with details of her plans to paint the vigas to match the wash n' wear wallpaper she has chosen, with a resplendent pattern of roses and vines, vines and roses.

I think of the cool whiteness of plastered walls, the functional simplicity of hand-adzed beams and try not to shudder. I look out her window at real flowers; the ones she wants on her walls have not yet leaped into her garden. I have run from plastic world; she has just entered it, an innocent. When I turn, her eyes search my face.

"Don't you like the color?"

"Umm, it's just that . . ."

"You should paint yours. You'll see. Someday cover up those old beams. So hard to dust."

How can I tell her what I really feel? How do I dare throw cold water on that blaze of creativity? I am a coward. I smile and praise the color and shine of Congoleum.

How could anyone ignore that expectant face beaming: "Won't it be beautiful?"

MARGARET RICE-JETTE

HEAT WAVE

The sheriff has gone, taking all the typed forms with him. Only the marks of tires are left in gravel. The old man and the old woman still stand, staring at nothing, on the edge of the garden under a hot brass sky.

They do not believe because they cannot believe.

All over the valley tomatoes are ripening on the vines too early, leaves already wilting to sick yellow. The corn is short this year, seeking moisture close to earth. Even now fields are alive with grasshoppers, taking what the drought has left. If this heat wave is not soon broken the fruit will be small and bitter. Except for hardy petunias, flowers are no more than brittle stalks burnt by three months of noon sun and no rain. Every two weeks a thin stream snakes down from Nambé, from the *Acequia Baranca*. But not enough to save the vegetable gardens.

The old man and the old woman have planted their garden in this spot each year for many years. They have always planted wisely, not by following the directions on seed packages, but according to their deeper knowledge of the land—land that has been good to many generations of their family.

The old couple seem curiously indifferent to the condition of the garden. They are staring at a dust devil winding its miniature tornado across the road. One more layer of sifted adobe sticks to the surviving hollyhocks.

They hear the car before they see it coming around the bend. Both turn in one motion toward it, almost recognize it, for one moment, think it is his car. The V-8 engine and no muffler—the low rider. Now they can see it cruising along at ten miles an hour in the center of the road. The young man with an arm around his girl, slouched behind the wheel. Stereophonic speakers blast hard rock over the valley—"Oh, baby, baby, baby . . ."

The car passes, evaporating to shimmer. Ghosting. Lost in white heat rising from the dry riverbed. The old ones stare after it with hungry eyes, because it is like their son's car, because it is the first thing that has moved in this heat since the sheriff's car came down the road and into their drive earlier this afternoon. Anything that can keep them from thinking of that is a good thing.

Sound from the vanished car seems to be pasted on the air in front of them—streamers of "Oh, baby, baby, baby . . ." their baby, the youngest, now grown—grown up baby.

If they stand very quiet and very still, and don't speak it aloud to one another, if they stand here propped up by the sun, their bones will deny it, grow warm again. Or turn into twin gnarled Russian olives, like the two old trees leaning intertwined in the lower field's irrigation ditch, the ones that shelter the pair of hawks.

She notices the neighbor's cat creeping up by the corner of the house, stalking hummingbirds under the flame colored poppies. Just now she cannot seem to raise arms, clap hands and shoo it away. A lizard scuttles over her sandal. She can feel it on bare flesh, at her foot's instep, but that's separate from her leg and has nothing to do with her. She looks down at her foot curiously, dispassionately, as if it were some strange stone turned over when she last spaded the garden.

He hears the "caw, caw" of crows overhead. Those crows will start on the corn soon. He is thinking that he should get some buckshot first thing tomorrow. Tomorrow . . . . . He rubs a big veined hand back and forth idly over the lower part of his jaw. Feels the stubble beginning to push through. "No, they're wrong. Wrong," he mutters. His son is going to help him with the second cutting of alfalfa tomorrow—in the north upper field.

When they can finally move, they move together toward the back screen door. He notices as it swings shut that the hinges need oiling—thinking it strange to been noticing such small things at a time like this. By some unspoken agreement they do not stop in the large sunny kitchen, but move on into the small formal room where gusts are usually entertained. They sit close to each other on the green sofa under the large collection of family photos.

She picks up one of the pillows, hugging it against her stomach, rocking slightly back and forth, unaware that she is moving. He notices, reaches out his hand, touches her shoulder. She stops. They sit in silence, bent in half, current between them too taut for speech.

She is thinking of the family photos on the wall behind them. Whenever she looks at them it seems to her that family is a long deep river, extending backwards far as time itself, extending forward where she cannot follow. But always flowing because of the two of them. She cannot put it into words, not to him, not even to herself. But when she feels this, it fills her heart.

"Can't think of that now. Can't think."

She gets up stiffly. They have been sitting there for a long time. Hours, it seems. She goes to the kitchen, makes the ritual coffee. Dries each cup afterwards as if it were a separate gem. As if the perfect roundness of edges makes her feel safe as that unbroken circle. She puts meat on to stew, moving automatically, setting out the already made *salsa*, the refried beans, the left over *posole*.

Coming to the bedroom, she comes out carrying her purse and a lace scarf. Speaks to him a moment in the small living room where he still sits. He nods but does not speak. Covering her head with the lace, she leaves for Mass—walking the two miles. Dust from the road whitens her black shoes, her dark stockings at the ankles. Afterwards, she will find someone to drive her home.

He sits on the *portal*, waiting for her to return. Rocking, rocking, staring toward the sinking light behind the cottonwoods, thin shanks scraped by peeling edges of cane, the chair he always intends to mend.

At supper he finally speaks.

"I should have stopped him—not let him have his way all the time."

He is thinking of other times, not just today.

"Come, you must eat. . . . No, no, not your fault. Not anyone's fault but his. It's in the hands of God."

If she says that to herself often enough she might begin to believe that this is so. She reaches for his hand.

They go to bed early, hoping sleep will come, a curtain to blur pain.

The moon unwinds. Full, plump with heat. Silvers flat leaves against the window. The moon whirrs, the clock in the hall, painted with strawberries, strikes eleven, then twelve.

All the birds of her dreams are rattling midnight trees. Somewhere a child is calling. She tries to answer.

Striking one. She hears three, sleeps again.

Sheets are moist with the heat of their bodies. He grinds his teeth. Through her own sleep she hears a soft moan escape his lips—as if his heart was slipping through his teeth.

Waking fully, she goes to the kitchen, looks out at trees streaked against the hills in first light, pulls at the chenille robe, ridges of folded pink, ties it closer to her body.

As if that one simple act could shut out the dark.

MATILDA ROMERO

Matilda Romero is a life-long resident of the Espanola Valley, where she graduated from Santa Cruz High School. After raising six sons, she attended Highlands University where she received a degree in Early Childhood Education. She was a Head Start teacher for eighteen years and is now retired. At present she is writing her memoirs, primarily for her grandchildren. She occupies much of her time creating in straw applique, a traditional New Mexico Spanish-colonial art form.

THE CASE OF THE CUT PERCHA IN KANGAROO COURT
(El Cerco, La Percha, y La Vecina Mala)

One day I decided to transplant a silverlace vine against the fence in my backyard. With the help of my children, I dug up the vine from its old location and moved it to a spot where I thought it would look best from my kitchen window. The three of us positioned the plant in the hole, filled it with soil, watered it, and guided some of the vines up the fence. After completing our gardening project, we stood back to admire the pretty green vines clinging to the fence wires. I visualized the day when it would fill the whole back fence with pretty white blooms.

Suddenly *La Vecina* came running from her house about one hundred feet away. As she approached, we heard her yelling: "Get away from my fence! Get away from my fence!" The children and I looked at each other, somewhat puzzled, then looked at La Vecina. She was yelling at the top of her voice, claiming that the fence was hers and warned us not to touch it. She yelled at us, saying that the fence belonged to her and that we were trespassing if we touched it.

I stayed calm, explaining to her that the fence was ours since my grandfather had put it up many, many years ago. I continued to explain that according to local tradition, if the posts were on my side of the property, then the barbed wire would be nailed to the side of the fence closest to her property. Traditionally, that is how one can tell which property owner originally built the fence. I remember my grandfather cut the posts from trees growing along *la acequia* that ran through his property. My grandfather, a real traditionalist, had explained this custom to me when I was a little girl.

I figured that because she had moved here from the East Coast she didn't know much about fences here in the Southwest. My attempt to educate La Vecina about local customs regarding fence ownership did not go over very well.

Next thing we knew, she pulled the green leaves from the vines, threw them on the ground and stomped on them. She was yelling and pulling and stomping . . . yelling, pulling and stomping the beautiful vines that my children and I had just planted!!!

El Vecino heard her screaming, as did everyone else in the neighborhood. He came running, grabbed his wife by the arm and pulled her away from the fence. La Vecina continued to scream "It's my fence! It's my fence!" till she was out of sight.

My children were shocked by her temper tantrum; they were shaken by all the screaming and antics of La Vecina. My children said that she looked like a *gallina culeca* as she paced back and forth, screaming at us and yelling obscenities and threats. After this incident, my children referred to the neighbor lady as "*La Vecina Mala*" and sometimes as "*La Vecina Loca.*"

My children and I looked at the torn leaves and destroyed vines sprawled on the ground on the other side of the fence. It made us very sad to see our work destroyed, My sons asked me why La Vecina was acting that way since they had never witnessed that kind of behavior before. For lack of a better explanation I answered: "Guess La Vecina wasn't feeling very well today." We left the shredded plant and walked away slowly and quietly.

Having put the incident aside, I proceeded with my usual chores. About thirty minutes later, I finished a load of laundry and hung my wash out to dry on *la percha*. La Percha just happened to be tied to one of the fence posts near the wilting silverlace vine. The clothes were flapping gently back and forth in the summer breeze when all of a sudden along comes La Vecina Mala again, running back to the fence. She took out a pair of wire cutters from her apron pocket and proceeded to cut la percha from the fence post. She worked very fast and before I knew it, she managed to cut down la percha. All my laundry came tumbling down. When I looked out I saw my freshly laundered towels and sheets laid out on the ground, still attached to la percha. That was the second time in one day that La Vecina had destroyed my day's work.

When I went out to see what all the commotion was again, La Vecina Mala was standing at the fence yelling profanities and proclaiming that the fence posts and fence belonged to her. El Vecino came out again and hauled her away again as she continued to yell at the top of her lungs, claiming ownership of the fence. Once again my children were puzzled by such bizarre behavior. We were very sad to see such a disturbed and agitated person. I just shook my head and we all went back into the house. The children asked if they should pick up the clothes from the grounded percha.

Luckily I had a Polaroid camera. I took pictures of the cut percha and my laundry lying on the ground. The next day my husband and I drove to the county court house and filed a complaint against La Vecina in magistrate court.

On the day of the hearing, La Vecina showed up late. When she did arrive, she made such a grand entrance into the courtroom that it took her what seemed like a lifetime to approach her seat at the front. She was dressed in her Sunday best.

She walked through the door assisted by a walking cane and her husband, who accompanied her at every step. Based on La Vecina's appearance, the impression she was attempting to make, for the benefit of the judge, was that of an innocent, frail little old lady who was too weak to do the things we said she had done. If this was the judge's initial impression, it did not last long. The judge (a justice of the peace) would soon get a taste of her medicine.

He started by asking her why she had cut la percha. Her answer was because the clothes line was tied to her fence post. After more deliberations and photo proof of La Vecina's actions, the judge found her guilty of destroying property and imposed a fine.

At that point La Vecina Mala proceeded to proclaim the judge's decision invalid. After the judge asked her to conduct herself in a respectful manner, she yelled out that she was not going to adhere to any decision made in a kangaroo court. Startled by her behavior, one of my sons asked, "What is a kangaroo court?"

At the judge's request, La Vecina Mala's husband quickly escorted her out of the court. This time it took her only a fraction of the time to walk the length of the courtroom. Needless to say, the interest generated by her entrance did not compare to the excitement she generated by her exit. Her accusations of being tried in a kangaroo court could be heard throughout the whole courthouse. As my husband, children, and I left the courtroom, I looked over to one side. I saw La Vecina's walking cane lying on the floor. I thought about my percha.

JOE E. ROMERO

Joe E. Romero, a New Mexico native and World War II veteran, is a retired business agent, Painters Local Union 869 in Santa Fe. He served as Labor Representative to the New Mexico District Council #63 in Albuquerque for over twenty-five years. Joe participates in various community activities and projects. Of noteworthy mention is his fifty years of dedicated service to the local community acequia/ditch association. His hobbies include wood carving, gardening, and volunteering for the Santa Cruz Senior Center.

LA VECINA MALA (THE MEAN NEIGHBOR)

Episode I: "Ain't Got No Chicken Feed!!"

It was just another day but the need to go to the grocery store arose and off I went without a care in the world. I felt relaxed, confident and in fact, cheerful. Never had I dreamed about what was about to happen to me.

As I walked down the aisle in pursuit of my designated purpose, I was stunned to hear what I thought was a gentle and inquiring voice asking if I was "Joe," and without thinking, I replied, "Yes I am." As I turned around to face the person, I was surprised to recognize *La Vecina*. All hell seemed to break loose. She started ranting and raving, pointing her fingers and moving in all directions, hollering at the top of her voice: "YOU are the one that has been stealing my chicken feed!"

I was completely dumbfounded and amazed at such an accusation. I tried to reason with her. I told her I didn't even have chickens and had no need for chicken feed and that perhaps she was in error.

She wasn't about to listen to what I had to say, but she continued from aisle to aisle, gesturing and hollering and repeating her accusations. I had never felt so embarrassed in my whole life. I left my shopping cart and walked to my vehicle to regain my composure and to assess my situation, as I was shaking and shivering. I finally drove home, told my wife all that had happened *and without the groceries!*

Episode II: Gun Wielding Neighbor—La Pistolera

There would be other incidents involving La Vecina, as her property was serviced by the community ditch, of which she was a member.

Community ditches (*acequias*) have a long history of being the lifeblood of the community, providing water for the purpose of growing agricultural products.

Community ditches for years have established easements or right of ways through the properties it services in accordance with state laws. The governing body of the ditch system is composed of three commissioners and one mayordomo, elected by the participants and landowners. The mayordomo is executive officer of the ditch and is in charge of the distribution of the water.

Early one morning the mayordomo knocked at my door all shook up and quite agitated, *"Vamos con migo, esa vieja cabrona no me deja echar el agua."* He was telling me, that old lady didn't let him turn the water on. He went on further as to what was happening and I suggested that perhaps we should invite another neighbor and landowner as a witness in case La Vecina decided to make good on her threats to the mayordomo.

The next door neighbor was more than glad to accompany the two of us. As we approached the main gate at the ditch, we could hear La Vecina yelling and making motions with her arms. We ignored her and continued with our assignment. The neighbor and I stood by while the mayordomo proceeded to open the head gate.

It didn't take long before La Vecina with pistol in hand, accompanied by her husband, approached us at the head gate. The mayordomo was still in the process of securing the head gate when two shots rang out and the bullets hit the water right in front of the mayordomo.

The mayordomo was a gutsy middle-aged man and wanted to take them on. I suggested that this was a case for the law to handle. They both agreed and we headed to the county courthouse in Santa Fe to file a complaint. Her day in court was a loss to her and her appeals were denied.

Episode III: The Ditch Witch

We thought that perhaps La Vecina had learned her lesson on that encounter, though she had gotten off easy. It wasn't long before we were faced with a similar problem involving the ditch on her property. As it happened, La Vecina in prior years had covered the whole ditch area with boards and the boards were now rotting and breaking away, causing the water in the ditch to overflow. The only solution was to open the ditch channel to remove the obstructions and repair the area. La Vecina would have nothing of that and told us that we were trespassing, that she had covered the ditch and that it was HER ditch. This time we got the community involved. We thought that perhaps La Vecina would listen to other members of the community in trying to resolve the problem, but to no avail. We chose a day for the neighborhood to get together. We notified the sheriff's department and they came on that day and the job got done over the objections of La Vecina Mala.

RON ROMERO

Ron Romero is a recently retired public health dentist. Ron served as New Mexico's Dental Health Director focusing on improving the oral health status of New Mexicans through the provision of dental care to the state's under-served populations. Dr. Romero continues to be active in dental public health through the American Public Health Association.

HALLOWEEN WITH LA VECINA MALA

The month of October was the longest month of the year. I would count the number of days leading up to what I felt was the most important day of the year—Halloween. I would stare at the old Rexall calendar hanging on the kitchen wall next to where we kept the house keys, as if to encourage time to move faster. Instead, it seemed to move slower. In my mind I crossed off each day, memorizing horoscopes, the daily weather, and all other information on the old drug store calendar. Day by day went by. Dad's birthday was in mid-October and my mine was on November 1, the day after Halloween and All Saints Day. I looked forward to my birthday but Halloween came first. These two events seemed to help me get through the month. I remember hearing my brothers exclaim, " You should have been born on Halloween, instead of All Saints Day."

On this particular Halloween I was more excited than other

years. Instead of the usual home-made outfit, I received a hand-me-down, store-bought costume from a relative who was now too old for Trick-or-Treating. I proudly wore my new-to-me skeleton costume to school for the Halloween party but did not tell any one that it was a hand-me-down, instead I said I got it at the local J.W. Owens 5 & 10 Store. Don't know if my classmates believed me because much of the silver glitter which formed the bones of the skeleton had fallen off. I didn't care if they didn't believe me or not. A store bought costume was a real treat in those days.

On Halloween night the neighborhood kids, my brothers and I would meet across the street at the local motel, which had a trailer park adjacent to it. This was a good place to start and depending on how it went, we would know how many other houses we needed to go to—to fill up our bags with candy.

Not having such a good year, the gang said, "Let's go over to La Vecina's house." Instinctively, my brothers immediately yelled out, " NO WAY!" Unfairly speaking for me, my brothers told the neighborhood kids to go ahead and go, but *we* could not go. My brothers said that we would wait for them and repeatedly told them that we were not allowed to go to La Vecina Mala's house. Kids being what they are, they wanted us to join them. They convinced us that La Vecina would not be able to tell who we were because we all were wearing masks and costumes. "Besides that," they said, "She usually gives out a lot of candy." That made for a convincing argument for an eight year old. Reluctantly, giving in to group pressure, we decided to give it a try. What the heck, it couldn't hurt.

The gang of kids went to the door and rang the bell. The porch light went on and La Vecina walked out. We shouted out the usual Halloween chant, "TRICK-OR-TREAT." La Vecina was surprised to see such a large group, about ten of us. She invited us to step onto her porch where she could get a better look. We did, and she then proceeded to ask each of us, one by one, to remove his mask and asked who we were. As this was going on, my brothers and I slowly inched our way to the back of the crowd. She allowed each child to step into her house after identifying him. I'm not sure why we just didn't turn around and leave before she got to us. I suppose we were caught by surprise. I remember being so scared that I couldn't move from hiding behind my two older brothers. When she got to us, hindsight should have told us to make up names, but the good children that we were, we told her that we were the neighbor kids and pointed to our house. La Vecina's whole attitude changed immediately. She told us to wait outside and slammed the door in our faces. It took a while for her to come back. When she did, she opened the door and threw one apple into each of our bags with such an angry force that I thought she was going to tear my brown paper bag and my candy would fall to the floor. I was not fast enough to get it out of the way—the apple flew into my bag as she yelled out to us, "The nerve of you kids coming here. Don't you ever come back again!" The door slammed once more. As we left, the other kids were still inside La Vecina Mala's house and I thought of Hansel and Gretel's fate. Low and behold that did not happen. They came out with big smiles on their faces, boasting that La Vecina had filled their bags with lots of candy—no apples.

At this young age, I was not yet prepared for life's lessons.

ANDRES U. ROMERO

Andres Romero is a life-long resident of Santa Fe. He retired after twenty-six years and eight months with state government on December 31, 1998. Since then he has devoted much of his time and energy to working with seven nonprofits. His hobbies include history, oral history and photography. Andres is currently working on four video documentaries, including an oral history of Word War II, the Low Riders, and the youth mariachi movement.

A MEMORABLE DAY

It was a beautiful Sunday morning in the month of May, way

back then. The azure sky was ever so clear and great excitement permeated the air like the welcome aroma of spring flowers. All of us first graders from the Saint Francis Elementary School, then located kitty-corner from St. Francis Cathedral, were gathered outside the three story brick school building in a group. The little boys standing nervously in their dark suits and little bow ties and the angelic looking little girls in their white veils and dresses. This was a special day. This was the day of our first Holy Communion. We were all marched in a single file into the church and seated up front for all to see. The little boys were seated on the right side of the aisle and the little girls on the left. The church was filled to capacity. It seemed that the whole town was there, including our parents, our uncles and aunts, and our many cousins and family friends.

I remember that after being seated one of the sisters told me, very explicitly, to concentrate on the little box on top of the altar. "That where God is at," she said, very matter-of-factly. Later on I was to learn that this little box was called a tabernacle. For almost an hour I never took my eyes off of the little box, while at the same time calculating that this God-Person had to be very tiny in order to fit in such a small space.

After we received communion and the mass ended, one of the supervising sisters gave a signal and the little boys started filing out of the church on one side of the aisle and the little girls on the other. Since I stubbornly refused to move from my seat, one of the sisters came up to me and proclaimed in a stern whisper, "Andres you have to move, we have to leave the church!" After a very long pensive moment, I pleadingly responded, "But sister, I am waiting to see God . . . . He has to come out of that little box for air and that is when I will finally get to see him!"

Thus began my innocent and very naïve journey at understanding the mysteries of the universe.

TOM HAMILL

Donna,
Tom Hamill

A New Englander by birth and a New Mexican by adoption, artist Tom Hamill has lived in Santa Fe since the mid-1960s. With a bold style that fuses realism with abstraction, Hamill's large oils depict the Maine mountains and the New England coast. He is a graduate of Bowdoin College who later studied at the Art Students League in New York and at the Skowhegan School of Art in Maine.

A DAY THAT A SOFA WAS SAWED IN TWO

I lived on Canyon Road for twenty-five years. Willa Palou was my landlady, a wonderful, generous lady. We were close friends. During the seventies the hippie invasion occurred. Willa had two rental houses besides the one she lived in. I lived in one. The remaining one was rented by a couple of St. John's students.

All went well until Willa noticed that this unit was visited endlessly by young people, hippies, at various hours. I noticed it, too, and grew suspicious. One day she heard a hand sawing noise from this house. She thought it strange and called me. I hadn't heard it because my house was in back. I went over to Willa's and we both knocked on the door of the suspected house. The door being unlocked, we entered.

The fumes of drugs were overpowering. But what was shocking was the sofa. It had been sawed in two. The couple were giggling and sitting on the parts, with the saw and sawdust in between, proud of what they had done.

"Why did you do it?" I asked.

"We wanted to make a love seat."

It was a life draining experience for us both. Poor Willa, who had not been well, had to be supported. We called the police, who had been staking out the house, to come at once and arrest the couple who had been dealing and using drugs. They paid for the sofa and vanished to jail, never to attempt to saw another sofa. Hopefully.

TOM HAMILL

FINN O'HARA VERSUS CLAUDE: An Incident at
Claude's Bar

Claude James owned a bar on Canyon Road, a meeting place for
a cross section of Santa Fe. Everybody came to it. It was a "mixed
bag of assorted cookies." Claude was an incredible woman—
gifted, raised in Paris and New York, migrated to Santa Fe—with
a charismatic and unique personality.

Finn O'Hara was one of the "assorted cookies." He was one
of those talented failures, an alcoholic who wasted his talents.
But he had charm and was liked, but had a bitter and acid tongue.
Claude didn't like him and vice-versa.

Then came a Saturday night, bar packed to the rafters, all the
"cookies" plus Hal West and me, and then it happened! Finn was
drunk and so was Claude. She was holding forth with tales of
Parisian life. Then Finn moved in, not wanting to be upstaged.
He insulted her. His back was to the wall and Claude, who had an
arm like my thigh, swung at him. He ducked and her fist hit the
wall with a loud THWACK!

The bar became silent as a tomb.

Finn said, "Is that your best shot, Claude?"

Finn was ushered out quickly and didn't appear for some time.
Next day, Claude with a bandaged right hand was her usual self.
That was her gift. Nothing fazed this remarkable woman, my dear
friend.

TOM HAMILL

TOMMY MACCIONE

Tommy Maccione had been born in Sicily and lived there until he

came to New York City about the 1930s. He studied art at the Art
Students League and then moved to Santa Fe. He had about
twenty-three dogs and two were always limping. He never had
any money and sold his paintings occasionally. Years later the
city supported him after taking away his dogs, for hygienic rea-
sons.

One day I saw him in Tito's Market, trailed by two dogs only.
He spotted me and said joyfully, "I sold a painting." I congratu-
lated him and looked into his cart. I saw one large T. Bone steak
and four cans of Alpo dog food.

I said, "You're going to have a big steak dinner tonight!"

Then he said, very seriously, "No, that steak is for my dogs.
The Alpo is for me. It is quite good."

I was surprised but I knew he was serious. That evening he
and his dogs had a delicious meal.

FRANCINE FRIEDMAN

*Francine Friedman is a psychotherapist by profession and a writer
by passion. Originally from New York City, she has lived in Santa
Fe for thirty-six years and has weathered many changes to the
city that pass for progress. She is also a jewelry historian because she needed to work with things beautiful and silent.*

SANTA FE IN THE SEVENTIES

Nineteen seventies Santa Fe certainly had its share of characters.

The Camera Man was an elderly gent who lived in my neighborhood on Don Gaspar Ave. He was, at best guess, in his seventies. Summer and winter, he wore a drab overcoat and a hat with
earflaps that were always down. He also wore two cameras around
his neck, the old-fashioned accordion-pleated type. Every afternoon he would walk to the camera store opposite La Fonda Hotel
and ask, "Are my pictures ready?" and every afternoon he was
politely told, "No sir, you'll have to come back tomorrow." Need-

less, to say, there was never any film in either camera.

Rubber Lady was an "artiste." She was dressed head to toe in what looked like a black wet-suit and had two inner tubes around her waist. Her face was also covered in something latex-ish. You would see her either draped around a lamp post or standing on the Plaza frozen in an artful pose. No one ever found out who she was but the story goes that the police gave her a ticket for something like '"disturbing the peace" and she was never seen again.

Pablito was short with a round sun-weathered face that made him look like a dried apple. He was Super-Christian. He would walk around the Plaza with a Bible in his hand and stop anyone he could, quote some scripture and sing a few hymns. This took about half an hour and it was nearly impossible to get away. More often than not, if he saw a woman walking alone he would stop her and tell her: "You are a whore." After being his victim one time too many, I told him to watch his mouth and he never came near me again.

Winnie Beasley was a hero and a character. Watching her tool around town in her vintage motorcycle complete with sidecar was a vision. She also wore an aviator's cap complete with goggles. Winnie was a pilot and carried mail during WW II. It was clear that she was reluctant to give up that exciting part of her life. Winnie had a stroke sometime in the eighties and one of her sons took care of her and the beautiful horse ranch they had in Tesuque, a small village five miles north of Santa Fe.

Horace Aiken was Winnie's opposite. When I knew him, Horace was in his eighties and had an apartment in La Fonda Hotel. Rumor had it that he was a remittance man. Mr. Aiken was always impeccably dressed for his daily constitutional in a homburg and navy pin-striped suit, red bow tie and white shirt with frayed cuffs and collar. He carried a silver-topped walking stick.

A bit later on, Skirt Man came on the scene. He was a Viet Nam vet who walked the Santa Fe streets in an army jacket, combat boots, knapsack and skirt. His choice of skirts was fairly ordinary except for the white satin wedding gown which he seemed to favor. The local newspaper did a small story on him in which he maintained skirts were much more comfortable than pants. Skirt Man was a vehement protester against nuclear weapons and would go up to Los Alamos, home of the atom bomb, to voice his opinions.

It was important to stand down-wind if you ever encountered Stinky Sam. Sam came from an affluent Pittsburgh family and was an antique dealer before succumbing to schizophrenia. He was also a remittance man. He lived in a storage unit—his girl-friend lived in an adjoining one—and conducted the business of buying and selling jewelry as he went from one store to the next. Sam, regardless of his non-existent hygiene, was one of the most honest people I've ever met. At that time I had a small booth in an antique mall. I always let him take a piece of jewelry from me if I felt he could make a few bucks and he always came back a few days later either bringing the piece back or with money to pay for it. At last sighting, Sam was taken back to Pittsburgh be-cause his illness became more active.

We don't have characters in Santa Fe now. The city has grown and we have become more uptight so that street performers like Rubber Lady would not be tolerated. The seven-foot transvestite who frequented the old Safeway downtown, silently guarding the oranges, would be quickly and quietly dispatched to somewhere else. We have lost a lot of what made us The City Different and we have sadly become The City Same.

LIZ JEFFERSON

Transplant Liz Jefferson has lived in northern New Mexico for more than half a century. She came here in the 1950s to live and work in Los Alamos, where she taught dancing by session in various venues. When she remarried and moved to Española, she established her own dance studio. Her integration into New Mexico culture happened through other transplants. "Brinck" is the story of one such influential encounter.

BRINCK

John Brinckerhoff Jackson looked me in the eye with a direct approach that managed to be both gracious and honest. Dressed in felt cowboy hat and leather boots, blue jeans braced with a leather belt latched with a silver buckle and a turquoise stone, we were almost eye to eye.

"Hello, and how are you?" he asked.

Landscape Magazine was advertising for a part-time person to assist with circulation. A Canyon road address. Editor and publisher, John Brinckerhoff Jackson. A magazine business housed in a two-room, adobe-looking building, certainly not a corporate establishment. I was face to face with *the* John Brinckerhoff Jackson. Brinck was a professor at Harvard and UC Berkeley. Fluent in languages, he spoke seven, as I recall.

A brief interview covered the basic skills needed. Business Manager Sylvia Loomis was in the room and part of the interview. Even then Sylvia was gray haired and had the demeanor of a purse-lipped maiden lady. She was far from that. Sylvia was a Quaker. Socially and philosophically she was a liberal, walking around in grandmotherly-like gathered cotton skirts and flat shoes. I soon realized that her soft-spoken manner disguised a will of steel.

My own flat Midwestern voice, tailored suit and hose covered a pedestrian attitude that did not blend with the general atmosphere. We stood there, all aware my outlook was different from theirs. Would our personalities blend at work? Brinck's New Jersey accent, Sylvia's soft spoken demeanor, and my own unadorned pragmatic expressions were to form an unlikely trio.

"The job is part time," Brinck informed me, "six hours a week. Magazine circulation is about three thousand and you would be responsible for the mailing."

Sylvia asked: "Can you prepare the mailing list, and update the subscriber information?"

Armed with resume, work skills, and experience, I answered, "Oh yes."

Brinck decided I would be added to the staff.

"Sylvia is business manager and your position is circulation manager."

Editor, business manager and circulation manager, all work was part time and all had titles. Operation of the business affairs was assigned to Sylvia and to me.

Brinck was concerned that *Landscape Magazine* project a professional appearance. Its covers were a blend of interesting photography with glossy exterior and creative type styles to project sophisticated literature. The polished veneer provided a bold introduction and insight into the content.

La Cienega was a small community near Santa Fe. Local residents were mostly Spanish. A small and active community, local fiestas and celebrations were routine. J. B. became a patron to La Cienega, sponsoring events and projects for resident families. His decision to build a swimming pool became a time consuming project. Dealing with business details caused him to pace in and out, back and forth, muttering to himself and talking to us. The land, dimensions of the pool, dealings with the local advisors and contractors were interruptions and intrusions on his academic pursuits and interests.

Interested in people from all cultures and walks of life, Jackson took every opportunity to talk with everyone around him. A visit over Danish in his kitchen was interrupted by a young local woman knocking on his back door. Immediately he began assessing some papers she showed him. He counseled her on classes. His manner was that of financier and professor. Quietly observing them, I had an image of him sitting on the steps at UC Berkeley in jeans, hat and boots, with intense face, a student by his side, gently guiding her thought in good directions.

Inquiries about my life were interspersed with our office conversations. A busy year 1959. My marriage was ending. My sister was getting married in my Santa Fe home. I needed legal advice concerning my divorce. Without being asked, Brink provided that. Next he asked about the wedding—where, when, and those involved.

My mother arrived early for the wedding. Immediately Brinck invited the bride and groom, mother and me, to his ranch for dinner. A gracious host and excellent cook, Brink did it all. Totally organized, the dinner was on the stove, and the scent of old fashioned cooking filled the house. Included with the hors d'ouerves was an invitation to view his private pond. It was Jackson's routine to skinny dip in the pond each morning, which was recessed in an area of green meadow, surrounded by trees. The groom accepted the invitation. Quiet and inviting, the water's temperature was refrigerator level. The groom came back to the dinner party looking pale blue, wondering if four days to his wedding night were enough to recover.

Brinck received the wedding invitation and asked, "Martha, I'd like to come to the wedding. Do you mind if I ride my motorcycle?"

"Arrive on whatever," I responded. "Just come."

He explained further: "On Sundays I ride my cycle to northern New Mexico to chart points of interest and inspect roads."

I still have a vision of him standing on the entryway of my adobe-looking home in Casa Alegra. Eyes wide, observing this mostly Los Alamos working class group, motorcycle parked among the cars. Attending the church ceremony then the reception, it was a world of people and conversation with which he had little familiarity. The abundance and quality of the gifts, the humor and easy conversation intrigued and amazed him.

Our working relationship changed as my life changed. As I divorced, remarried and had a child, we lost contact for a number of years. In my dotage I decided to go to college. The best advice around would come from Brink Jackson. I telephoned him.

"Of course," he said "come on Thursday at 10:00 a.m."

We met and he welcomed me as if he had seen me yesterday. Of course we talked in the kitchen. An antique looking stove stood by the wall. Reaching for the teakettle, for a pan for muffins, for cups for coffee, he asked questions. Mulling over my responses, he provided insight and direction.

We made sporadic contact over the years as I visited New

Mexico family and friends. At times he revealed a little of his background, and finally that he was ill. In 1993 he received the Pen Award for a book of essays. I last saw him about 1995. Evidently ill but still mobile and alert, we talked intensely during the brief time we had. I learned of his passing via a clipping of his obituary. John Brinckerhoff Jackson is buried in the cemetery at La Cienega, the community he loved and lived in with gusto.

Always a life in transition, originally he was John Brinckerhoff Jackson, known as Brinck. Then he became J. B. Jackson. His last request of me was to call him John.

GERRY WOLFF

Born in San Francisco, educated at U.C. Berkeley and Stanford University in landscape architecture and urban and environmental planning, Gerry Wolff has recently relocated from the San Francisco peninsula to Santa Fe, where she is busy exploring her new environment and its inhabitants.

HENRY LUNA

Henry Luna lives in Mountainair, New Mexico, near the Manzano Mountains, about seventy-five miles southeast of Albuquerque. That is, he did when I met him in 1999, when I was visiting friends on their horse ranch, four miles out of town. Mountainair, on Route 60, had been the pinto bean capitol of the world in better agricultural times—before the soil was depleted. Mountainair, population plus or minus 1 thousand, has a downtown consisting of buildings from the 1950s and before, housing such institutions as The Cowboy Café, The Rosebud Saloon, and the town hardware store, where established citizens were noted by a display of their brands high on the wall, including that of Henry Luna.

I met Henry Luna during August, the hottest month of the year, when the rain pounds down periodically. He was doing work for the horse ranch owner, building a horse barn and sturdy fences in the typical New Mexico tradition—huge posts with wire. Henry Luna could build anything and make it into an art form—barns, fences, patios of New Mexico red flagstone. Even carve walking sticks from found nature-shaped wood inlaid with found Indian arrowheads. He would search out pieces of local wood that he thought had potential and would make the most of their unusual shapes. He was an artist, although he had had no art training. Henry Luna was very observant, a fast learner, a natural artist.

Henry Luna—slight-in-build, not tall, about forty years old. Always dressed in cowboy boots, black cowboy hat, yellow leather chaps. A walking photo op. Looked a bit like Santana, the famous musician, but Henry Luna was shorter and better looking. He was sort of an unelected mayor of Mountainair. People came to him to solve problems. Bright, a caretaker, he knew everybody. Yes, a natural problem-solver.

Henry Luna may be related to all the New Mexico Lunas, and many other families of New Mexico, as well. The town of Los Lunas was named for his relatives. (*"Luna"* means "moon" in Spanish). When I first passed Los Lunas I couldn't understand what I thought (in my limited knowledge of Spanish) was gender inconsistency. Shouldn't it be *Las Lunas,* the feminine plural? But *Los* (masculine) was referring to the relatives of Henry Luna, mostly male, I guess.

As I was without a car, I was not able to leave the horse ranch, where Henry Luna and his brother, Philip, were building a barn. One day they were framing the roof, another photo op. I photographed them in the air surrounded by boards and sky. As I approached them they changed their conversation from Spanish to English so I would not be excluded.

Their kindness was extended to an old man from Wisconsin, a white-haired anglo, resting in the bed of a compact dark blue Ford station wagon. They brought him with them to watch their work and to have company, and not be alone.

I approached the old man sitting in the car, and stood and talked with him for awhile. Henry Luna very quietly, without a word, left his roof-top perch in order to get a chair and silently place it next to me, so I could sit and talk.

I said to Henry Luna: "From your manners and the fact that you take responsibility for others I would guess that you and your family have been around here for a very long time."

He said, "We are related to the Duke of Albuquerque, who came from Spain to settle that city in 1706, hundreds of years ago. We have been here a very long time."

I never forgot it, and I haven't forgotten Henry Luna.

GERRY WOLFF

JOE/EXIT 299

It was early evening on the first working day after Christmas. I was alone, at a local fast food restaurant. I had been alone at Christmas as I was under the weather—not sick, but not quite well. Just exhausted from my recent move to my new Santa Fe house. It was okay to be alone at Christmas, as I had had many wonderful holiday celebrations in the past with family and friends, some of which I had hosted. Now I just like to have a quiet Christmas and see what happens, what unexpected expressions of friendliness will surprise me—the unplanned pleasant surprise is more fun to me than the planned hard work of entertaining others.

There were just a few customers at Blake's Lotaburger where I was quietly eating my single Lotaburger, chili bowl and vanilla shake. I noticed a man waiting for his order, no doubt similar to mine, as the menu-hamburger choice was single or double Lotsburger or single or double Itsburger (a bit smaller). He was obviously a local, I obviously was not. A middle-aged, shortish, bearded cowboy dressed in a handsome black cowboy hat. Spanish heritage with a touch of Danish. (I noted the blue eyes). With order in hand he asked me if he might join me. At another time I probably wouldn't have said, "Yes." At another time he probably wouldn't have asked. I said, "Yes, it's Christmas! Please sit down." Joe Sanchez sat down.

Joe said, "I talk a lot. I like to talk to people. Some people don't like it. If they don't like it, I just throw them a finger!" This man was lonesome. But at our age we are all a bit lonesome at Christmas, reminded of those we have lost.

Joe said, "I just quit a three-year job today and stepped right into another job. There was even *another* job waiting for me. I drive trucks and do construction work."

Joe needed to tell somebody, even a stranger, about his new beginning—so close to New Year's—our big annual new beginning.

We talked about respect. Where had it gone? He had taught his kids to be respectful and honest. "Remember when we used to leave our houses unlocked? Then just the back door unlocked? Then house and car locked, at all times? And now security systems!?"

We had both sadly experienced this change though in different parts of the country: he, in Glorietta, New Mexico at exit 299 off of Interstate 25, not far from Santa Fe. And I in another state.

We talked about horses. He had horses. "Do you know horses?"

"Yes, I know horses," I responded.

As a teenager I had competed in horse shows with my cow horses, Silver and Poppy, with some success. Joe just loved riding horses in the mountain wilderness. That's what he'd really like to be doing.

We both finished our Christmas Lotaburgers and readied to depart.

"If you ever want to ride horses in the mountains you can find me in the trailer next to the Catholic Church at exit 299. Merry Christmas." He waved.

"Happy New Year, Happy New beginning." I responded.

I may never see Joe Sanchez again, but I'll remember our brief visit sharing Lotaburgers and holiday cheer on that first working day after Christmas.

CLAIRE SIMPSON

Claire Simpson, one of a pair of twins, was born in New York City into a Jewish family deeply concerned with education. She attended Hunter High School, Hunter College and Smith School for Social Work, graduating with an MSS. Always a lover of language, she enjoys word play and all kinds of writing—letters, poetry, memoirs, fiction. She describes herself as a storyteller, happily unmarried and childless. At eighty-five, her memory has holes in it, but not for jokes which she loves and remembers. An iconoclast, she now lives in Santa Fe with two dogs and two cats.

YOU CAN'T TELL A BOOK

He looked so clean cut, so all-American. His name was Lars Anderson. He looked what I thought of as typically Scandinavian—tall with blonde hair and blue eyes, somewhat lanky with a brooding quality about him. Something strange and indefinable about him . . . always a turn on for me. And he wanted the apartment! He came with references, had a job, not much of a job, but a job, delivering flowers for Barton's.

Great. I hated interviewing tenants. He was the first and he looked good. He moved in fast and easy, not much furniture, but many guys in their thirties and forties seemed to live out of boxes. He paid first and last month. We put the deposit off for two weeks till next pay check. The apartment was small, but complete with a sleeping loft, a full kitchen and bath, self contained with its own entrance.

We shared the garage. His car was an oldie—big, light blue, neat. We helloed couple of times in passing.

The first Sunday I was ready to do the steps. They needed painting. I was gathering my stuff when he spotted me.

"Here, lemme help, ma'm," he offered. "Then maybe we can work a swap for the deposit. I'm a good painter."

I lowered the paint can and looked up. This was gonna be great. I smiled all over and handed over the stuff. If I could have

whistled, I would have. Released, I took the car, called up the
dogs and off we went to the dog park, to the market, to Julie's for
some of her hot pecan pie, the ice cream puddled around it.

Her house was mostly kitchen, the bumpy adobe and silverlace
vines typical of the old neighborhoods of Santa Fe. The small
bedroom was full of dresses, coats, balls of wool, patterns. Ev-
erything she touched with her magic became beautiful, tasted
wondrous. She was a force of nature, a magician, a bruja, always
welcoming, nurturing, a respite in the turmoil of my tumbled feelings about the new tenant, the strangeness of him, life in general
so far this century. As we sat, the kitchen darkened, the shadows
beckoning me home.

Aware that the darkness prevented the dogs and me from see-
ing if the steps were done, we went in the garage way, so we
wouldn't mark the wet. Sniffed for the paint smell... nothing.
The wind must have dispersed it.

Come morning my feet followed my thoughts to the steps.
Nothing. Opened the door, stood on the portico. Nothing.

"I don't get it. What happened?"

"I don't get it" ricocheted in my head. Back to bed I went,
comforter tight around me, back to sleep to wake up better. It
didn't work. I did what I could do . . . nothing. Nothing but wait
till he came home.

Around dinner time he knocked on the door. I was expecting
him.

"What's up?" I asked. "When are you starting?"

His face darkened, jaw tightened, body tensed. He seemed to
get bigger, to swell. His voice was deep, with a rustling sound
new to me.

"I'm getting ready. Don't worry," he said.

He was frightening. I tried a smile, offered him coffee. He
was too busy for coffee, had to work, would get back to me. Clos-
ing the door was a relief. Such anger emanated from him I feared
it might singe the door. It was a solid one. I was glad for that. I
just stood there a while, absorbing the feelings in bits, the info
that our tiny contact revealed.

My God, I thought, he's crazy, paranoid! I live alone. What have I gotten myself into?

From that moment, I was careful. I was dealing with a powder keg of fury, easy to ignite, better watch my step. He had a lease.

CARMEN CHAVEZ-LUJAN

Carmen Chavez-Lujan is a second generation Chicana, born and raised in El Paso, Texas. She is the proud mother of four children, Chacho, Andrea, Daniel and Alfonso and has a beautiful three-year old granddaughter, Lilliana. She got her Bachelor's Degree in English with an Extended Major in Spanish from Stanford University in 1982. She now resides with her children in Santa Fe.

"TIO"

Tío was not actually my *tío*. He was an old Chinese man who owned the Shanghai Grocery Store on Missouri Street in Sunset Heights in El Paso, Texas. The store has since been torn down to make way for the freeway. But all the neighborhood children called him Tío. His son Buck and Buck's wife, Sylvia, helped him run the store.

My mother would send me to the store for a loaf of bread or a pound of *carne molida* or whatever. Buck would grind the meat right in front of me. The store was across the street from where we lived. The house has been torn down too. Mom would always say, "Be sure to ask Tío for *pilon*." That meant to try to get something free, not to be mistaken for a five-finger discount. So I would run across the street and into the store.

Tío would be sitting behind the counter on his stool, usually falling asleep. Tío was fluent in Chinese and Spanish. He pretended to be a mean old man and he would glare at you when you came in. But the kids knew better. He would get me what I was sent for and put it on the counter. I would ask him to put it on our *cuenta* like my mom would say.

"Cuenta?" Tío would say. "What cuenta? You a clazy kid. When your momma gonna pay?"

Then I would say, "Tío, *pilon*?"

"Pilon? What pilon?" And then he would mutter something in Chinese, turn around and give me a loaf of day old bread or a bunch of overripe bananas and then he would tell me to go away.

I remember one day I did a very shameful thing and I have not confessed it until today. It was right before school started. Tío had all the school supplies behind the counter. He would let the kids go behind the counter and select their supplies. I grabbed some paper that day and I hid one and only paid for one. It cost a whole nickel. I got away with it, but I felt so guilty. I went back later and snuck the paper back on the shelf. I'm glad my mother never found out, because she would have spanked me for sure.

I was very sad when Tío died. He was a good man.

CARMEN CHAVEZ-LUJAN

REFLEJOS DE MI MADRE

Mom and I were as different as night and day. Or so I have thought all my life. How could I consider myself like my mother? Here I am a college-educated, "worldly woman." My mother, at best, got a third grade education, even though the last time I asked her she said she went up to the eighth grade. I do not know why she feels she has to lie about her education. She is still the smartest woman I know.

My mom, Alicia, was and still is a beautiful woman. She is five feet tall, in heels, slight of build and she has this wonderful crooked impish smile and every so often you can catch a mischievous glimmer in her eye. She walks with this air, straight and strong and commanding—such a presence. At least that is how I remember her. She was raised in El Paso, Texas, raised by my grandmother, Amalia, and her grandfather. At the age of ten, my mom had to go to work because my grandmother suffered a heart attack. She supported the family, which included her little sister Yolanda, for two years, until my grandmother married my step-grandfather, Salvy, who worked with the Southern Pacific Railroad, under the *Bracero Program.*

Mom married my father, Ruben, when she was seventeen years old. My father was sixteen. My brother, Luis, was born a year later. I asked my mother once what being married so young was like. She said, "Your dad and I got married at City Hall. When we got back, your grandmother Josefina grabbed his hand and took him home." You see, my grandmother did not like my mother much. She didn't think my mother was good enough for my dad. In truth, my dad was not good enough for my mother. And that's the truth as I see it. She didn't say anything else and I didn't ask her anything until many years later.

I asked, "Mom, if my grandmother took my dad home, how did you two get together and have children?"

She said, "We only lived around the block from each other." Enough said.

I remember my mom worked at W. T. Grants on Stanton Street for many years. She was a cashier. I loved going to visit her after school. She would always get me a chicken salad sandwich. She knew it was my favorite. Then, she would treat me to a butter pecan ice cream cone. I looked forward to those times.

While she worked, my Aunt Yoli or Aunt Mary would take care of us. She didn't make much money and my father only paid $20 child support for me and my brother. My father never paid child support for my little sister Ceci. When my mother divorced my father, I was four and my brother was six. My mother did not tell the judge that she was expecting my sister because she knew the judge would not have granted the divorce, if he knew she was pregnant.

My mother was petite, but she was tough as nails. She had to be to survive. She always tried to give the appearance of being a hard, unfeeling woman, but I knew better. At night, when she thought we were asleep, she would sit next to us and caress our faces or run her fingers through our hair.

I remember my Aunt Herlinda came over to our house one day. Now my Aunt Herlinda was something else. She was the matriarch of the family. When the kids saw *Tía* Herlinda coming up the steps, we would run and hide. My mother had to pull us out of the closet or from under the beds to come and greet Tía Herlinda. I was about twelve then. Mom and my Tía were having a heated conversation about I did not know what. They were speaking in pig Latin, rapidly and I just sat there quietly, amazed that they could hold a conversation in a foreign language.

"Efe stafa efe mefe bafa rafa safa dafa?" said my Tía.

"Nofo. Cofo mofo puefe defe defe cirfi efe sofo!!" said my mom.

I found out later that my Tía was asking my mom if I was pregnant, because I was wearing a loose-fitting blouse. Heck, I was only twelve and I was the *monja* to boot. My mom was enraged that my aunt could make such an accusation against her daughter who was destined to be a nun. But that's a whole other story.

My Tiá Herlinda was quite a character. She and her siblings all came over from Chihuahua, Mexico when they were younger. She married an Army officer, Oliver Beckham from Fort Bliss. She always thought she was better than everybody else because she married an "Americano." But she was darker than everybody else in the family. She would complain about the *Juarenas mojadas* who cleaned houses in El Paso. She said they were all a bunch of thieves. I was confused. How could my Tiá Herlinda, born in Mexico, darker than anyone, be so prejudiced. Don't get me wrong. She had a good side too. She just would not let it show too often.

She was jealous as all get out too. She lived in Missouri at one time when Oliver was stationed there. I heard there was a party which included dancing. My Uncle Oliver made the mistake of dancing with another woman. Tiá Herlinda pulled Oliver aside and took him into another room. Everyone was worried about my aunt because there were loud noises and furniture banging going on in that room. When my Aunt Herlinda came out, my Uncle Oliver followed close behind, black and blue from the thrashing my aunt had given him.

Even when Uncle Oliver died, she made sure that there was a man buried next to him and that her burial plot was on the other side of him. She said, "There will never be another woman between us!!" This is the type of woman I hail from.

Anyway, getting back to my mother, she was twenty-six when she got divorced. She chose never to marry again because she didn't want anyone mistreating her children. Not that she did not have the opportunity, she had plenty of suitors and she did have other relationships, mostly in California.

Every summer, we would all pack our clothes and hop on the train to Los Angeles. My grandfather worked for the railroad, remember, so we rode for free. We did not have suitcases then. We packed our clothes in cardboard boxes, real big ones, like the ones toilet tissue comes in. For the longest time, I thought this was the way everyone traveled. It was not until years later, when my brother was working, that he gave my mom a set of suitcases. This, in and of itself, was a status symbol – matching suitcases!

My cousin Elodia and her husband Jose owned a restaurant bar in Torrance. My mom, I am just guessing now, worked at Joe's Bar during those summers. That is where she made a lot of friends. She was very proper, however, except for a couple of times when she slipped up. That's when my brother Rey and sister Armi were born. She never committed though. Then, at the end of the summer, we went back to El Paso.

I heard a rumor once that my mom was going to marry someone from California. His name was Pete. He worked in a grocery store. But then there was a burglary and he was shot and killed. I get all my information piecemeal and I don't even remember the sources, but back then I wouldn't dare ask my mom. Maybe I'll get up enough nerve to ask her now.

DONNA PADILLA

A life-long resident of New Mexico, Donna Padilla moved to Santa Fe in 1953 where she still lives with her husband Tony, whose family has been in Santa Fe since the 1690s.

BOOMTOWN—NEW MEXICO

It was the early sixties and the beat generation was hanging out in coffee houses, listening to bongo drums and incomprehensible poetry. Before the decade was out teens would be dropping out, forming a counter culture, riding freedom buses, passing out flowers, and burning draft cards. I dropped out of college after two years, loaded all my worldly possessions in my beat-up old Buick and headed for a boomtown in southern New Mexico to stay with my sister until I could figure out my next move.

New Mexico was having an extractive heyday and boomtowns were springing up all over the state. This once quiet ranching town was now surrounded by trailer parks. Grazing land was dotted with pumpjacks bobbing up and down, sucking oil from underground basins. Skeletal drilling rigs towered over scrubby desert plant life. Miles and miles of new natural gas pipelines were being laid. Every other day pipes and industrial equipment were unloaded from flatcars, and gondolas were loaded with tons of potash. Mud trucks and water trucks paraded up and down main street, and parking spaces were filled with cars and pickups bearing out-of-state license plates.

Extractive industries usually run three shifts a day, so there is always one shift working, one shift sleeping, and one shift eating and drinking. Hotels, motels, bars, and restaurants are the real gold mines in any boomtown.

Work is always easy to find in a boomtown, and having had some bar experience while working my way through college, I set out to canvas the bars in town. Every bar was fully staffed, but each wanted a backup person to call when they needed an extra hand or when a bartender or waitress failed to show up. Within no time I found myself working almost every bar in town. It wasn't unusual for me to work the day shift in one bar and the night shift in another.

In the hotel bar one encountered company executives, local bigwigs, tourists, and the railroad crew that stayed over every other night. One night a bus carrying a college basketball team (mostly black) on its way home from a tournament stopped at the hotel. I was waiting tables and was very embarrassed when the bartender refused to serve the team. Martin Luther King was very far away in the South.

Red Adair and his crew headquartered in the hotel while working at extinguishing the well fire that turned night into day. I am proud to say that I have met Red Adair, the world renowned oil well fire fighter. Whenever the classic movie channel airs the film with John Wayne portraying Red Adair, I watch.

All the local good old boys hung out at the country-western dance hall and rode herd on the local good old girls. Women are always in short supply in a boomtown. Stetson hats and Wrangler jeans were the accepted dress. On weekends the parking lot was always filled with Ford and Chevy pickups, and it was not unusual for a rebel yell to rise above the amplified guitars.

A couple of bars catered to the boomers. Money changed hands over the pool tables, liars poker was played at the bar, and everybody always knew where the real poker games were. City and county coffers were strained, law enforcement officers worked overtime, and gambling laws were not high on the enforcement priority list.

It took me a while to figure out that there were at least three different kinds of poker games going on. One was the typical spontaneous game that people play on payday. Another was a twenty-four-hour-a-day, seven-day-a-week game in one of the motel rooms. The players changed as the work shifts changed. Finally, I discovered that there was a group of professional gamblers working around town. They never played two days in a row, never used the same location twice, and the games were by invitation only. There were spotters working for the professional gamblers in some of the bars, keeping their eyes open for people flashing wads and looking for action. These spotters had to have a sixth sense for personality because they could not afford to invite an undercover cop or a poor loser.

The one pro who played in every private game was the Midget, who seemed to have stepped off the page of a Damon Runyon short story. He was just a tad over five feet tall and always wore a white Stetson to hide his baldness. A diamond ring flashed on his left hand, and he called it his insurance policy. There was always a buck or two tucked into his custom-made boots because he never knew when he might need bail money. He had a construction job which took him to boomtowns, and he was a member of his trade union.

Eventually I managed to land a full-time bartending job. The clientele was a mixture of local blue collar and farm workers, documented and undocumented aliens. What held them together in common bond was the Spanish language. The bar was a drafty, unadorned barn-like structure with generic chairs and tables, a couple of pool tables, and a jukebox that blasted Mexican music. The bar ran halfway across one side of the room and was constructed of rough, unfinished lumber. The only access to the back bar was through the store room, and the only door in the store room led to the parking lot.

Bill, the owner/manager, had sustained a back injury while trying to break up a bar brawl and had very strict rules for his bartenders. They were never, never, never to cross to the other side of the bar. If something started going down, they were to go into the store room and lock the door behind them. They would then lock the front door from the outside and call the cops. Forget the bar. Take care of yourself.

One night I was pulling some draft beers and looked up to see about eight or nine cowboy hats coming through the front door. Knowing that this particular crowd usually drank Seagrams VO, I went to the store room to get a full bottle. Bill was there with his feet propped up, and when I reached for the VO he came to immediate attention and muttered, "Oh, shit." Knowing that the two groups now occupying the bar might not be an amicable mix, we discussed a couple of possible impending scenarios, then both went back into the bar. All the cowboy hats were lined up at the bar waiting for their drinks. There was nobody else in sight.

On Saturday nights we usually served a standing-room-only crowd, so I was backed up by a bouncer and a waitress. One particular Saturday night, about half way through the shift, I realized that the bouncer had given up and joined the crowd, and that the waitress was about half crocked. I was pulling drafts, opening beer bottles, and ringing the cash register as fast as I could, but not fast enough for one man standing at the end of the bar. He started by yelling, "*Cerveza, cerveza!*" Shortly, he began punctuating his yells by banging his empty bottle on the bar. Finally, in total frustration, in an attempt to get my attention, he hurled the bottle in my direction. It missed. All activity in the bar came to an abrupt halt. Nobody knew what my reaction was going to be. I marched to the store room, grabbed a broom, poked the offender in the chest with the broom handle and roared, "You broke it, you clean it up!" I never crossed to the other side of the bar. He did.

In the early 1980s I was back in the boomtowns, but this time as a socioeconomic consultant. Instead of opening beer I was carrying a briefcase. This time it was coal, power plants, and carbon dioxide. My associates could run statistical computer programs, produce charts and graphs, and sell impact mitigation plans to company executives and government agencies. My area of expertise was dealing with the local people. Regardless of the location and the reason for the boom, the problems are the same: inadequate infrastructure, an out-of-whack economy, and the strain of social adjustment. Town populations double, triple, and sometimes quadruple during a boom, but you don't want to overbuild the infrastructure because the bust will definitely come and a lot of ghost towns will be made.

Feelings always run high in boomtowns, and we are all apt to get caught up in the myth that we are experiencing something unique. There have always been large transient populations in America, and one need only visit an old gold mining ghost town from the 1800s to remember that fact.

DENISE LYNCH

Denise Lynch is a poet who lives in Galisteo where she raises and rides horses. Lynch traveled three continents and throughout the United States as a representative of Animal Ambassadors International. Her photography and writings owe much to the inspiration of St. Francis of Assisi and her Comanche Ancestors.

THE EAST SIDE OF SWEET

A journey we take when we eat something from childhood—
Our taste buds and teeth not quite grown—

Last week I ate a perfect candy apple,
Taste of the map of my mother:
Me as a young girl,

The old cash register, its ring from my little fingers,
The small currency inside, a ticket to Kaune's Food town,
Butterscotch—
The other east side stores—Canyon road grocery
And the green apple jolly rancher stick—

Tito's, marked up mercifully and far away—

Gormley's, the gangly organized couple who sold
The candy—

Dramatic husband and wife team on Palace Avenue
Who were used to the street club kids—

Scary Johnny's Cash Store perched on the roadside,
Cruelty of kids pretending to be dogs—sometimes the chance

To view: pickled pig's feet, large dills, jerky, chili chips, pork
skins-

They knew me at Christo Rey Grocery
My sweet tooth curiosity, sucking the sticks in plastic wrappers
Made our dirt roads more bearable—

From my front porch to that store I was
Every turquoise window, every sewer cap, every dog's voice.
Adobe walls held me as sports flew by—

My dog followed me—we entertained the tourists.

I had two childhoods: in one I was loved and free to explore,

The other, the dark star, Llarona of the river park,
Rush of sugar at twilight,

Five-pointed star in the apple core
My mother made in October

PRISCILLA HOBACK

*Priscilla Hoback lives in Galesteo, New Mexico, where she has a
ceramic studio, six Arabian horses, and a large garden. She is a
regional artist inspired by archetypal images, native clays, and
village life.*

JOEY & ELVIS

I had ten neatly folded twenty dollar bills stuffed deep in the pocket
of my jean jacket. This money had been carefully saved to buy a
horse of my own.

There were large cattle ranches north of Las Vegas on the
open grasslands, good horse country. Every spring ranchers sold

a few of the three-year-old colts.

I remember that Sunday afternoon so clearly, stepping carefully around clumps of dead yellow grass, a chilly spring wind made walking difficult and the sky was a brilliant blue. I had to squint my eyes against the glare. It was one of those vivid New Mexico days.

We walked downwind toward the small herd of horses. A sturdy buckskin colt caught my eyes. Born on this ranch, he had been bred to be a cow pony, his history and blood showed in the color of his buckskin coat and tiger striped legs. His eyes were bright with intelligence.

This was my first venture of "horse trading." I handed over one hundred fifty dollars. We shook hands, and I had my horse and money to buy a used saddle.

One of the cowboys got a rope on him. We pushed him, stiff legged and shaking into the old trailer and drove back to Santa Fe. On the ride home I named him Joey. Probably because I always loved the folk song, "Little Joe the Wrangler."

We were headed to a new stables on lower Alameda Street, next to the old World War Two interment camp.

Twenty miles away, you could see the twinkling lights of Los Alamos. Daily, Jack Blevans drove a big rig up and down the dangerous switch back road carrying building materials, but on weekends he and friends roped calves and helped build the Sheriffs Posse Stables.

This stable was the center of my universe for the next few years. I thought of it as my home, my school, my job and the most wonderful place imaginable.

This posse rode as a mounted troupe, dressed alike in elaborate turquoise shirts, black and white chaps with initials branded deep into the leather. Many collected beautiful silver studded saddles, bridles and the horses to wear them.

I remember the architect, Mr. Kruger, bought a beautiful, spirited palomino horse in California. This horse, Goldie, was parade and high school trained; he pranced and bowed and was so fancy and I was so smitten. Goldie opened a new world for me, one of show horses and trick training.

I grew up around cowboys and cowponies. I had worked several summers at the Bishops Lodge Dude Ranch, saddling horses and helping with trail rides. Now I was working with show horses, grooming and exercising them during the week to make the money that supported Joey and my pickup truck.

The wrangler who ran the barn was an old cowboy named Jim Bryant, recently released from the state prison on Cordova Road where he served time for robbing the Santa Rosa bank. Before he turned to crime, he had worked on a cattle ranch in Texas where he trained young horses. He had the wry gentlemanly manner that comes naturally to western men. He knew a lot about life, survival, men, and being on one's own. He took me under his wing. I was a sponge and probably learned some things he never meant to teach.

But he did want to pass on every thing he knew about horses. He showed me how to move slowly and speak softly around spooky horses, and to stay calm and always pay attention. He would coach me while leaning on the fence. "Feel his mouth, feel his feet." "You are so owl headed." Or "quit running with your tail up." He thought of horse training as a one, two or three cigarette problem. This meant: "Slow down for as long as necessary. Relax and wait."

Joey quickly responded to saddling, riding, shoeing and vigorous grooming. No more shaggy tangled hair or cockle burs on his shinny black tiger striped legs. I polished his coat till it shined like copper.

The posse members were very kind to me. They rewarded my hard work with encouragement, support, and occasionally presents. One of my most prized gifts was a leather hand tooled cup that attached to my right stirrup and securely held the flag pole. It is a proud thing to carry a flag horseback in front of the band.

There were many local rodeos in small towns called affectingly "pumpkin rollings." They were all pretty much the same. A parade through the center of town, a Saturday night cowboy dance, the dance hall decorated with twisted crepe paper streamers.

Pickup trucks with kids and dogs and blankets backed up to out-door arenas. Lots of local young men showing their skill, proving their courage and earning their manhood.

Rodeos began with the grand entry, the presentation of flags and the playing of the Star Spangled Banner. Posse members and contestants alike rode this serpentine parade. Often daddies carry their young children in front of the saddle and handsome cowboys rode double with their sweethearts.

Then begin the main events of bronc riding, steer wrestling, calf roping, and bull riding. Mid afternoon when they reloaded the bucking shoots with fresh stock there was a crowd pleasing competition for the ladies. Ranchers' daughters and rodeo queens compete in a Barrel Race.

I trained Joey to run and turn. Barrel racing suited him, he was quick, handy and sure footed. Competing in front of the crowds was something new, scary and tough on the nerves but one just 'cowboyed' up. Slowly, I rode better, ran faster and this thrill grew in my blood.

Joey was "cowpony fast" but not "thoroughbred fast." Often our winning times were made because he could turn on a dime and give you five cents change. When racing the stopwatch you need to hurry every chance you get. I carried a quirt and would swat him on the straightaway, but he ignored it most of the time. Being confident or perhaps a little lazy, and much too smart for his own good, he preferred tricks for treats. He preformed many of the very ones I first admired when performed by the palomino, Goldie.

Horses were welcome in Santa Fe then. Joey would jump into the bed of my pickup just like a big dog. We would go up San Francisco street, then around the plaza. There was a horse watering trough provided by the city next to the library. One time on a dare, a double dog dare, a friend and I rode into the Hotel La Fonda lobby, stepping gingerly up steps and across polished *saltio* tiles and then on into the bar. We were graciously asked to leave.

I remember being at Berts Burger Bowl one afternoon with Joey in the pickup. I can clearly see my friends wearing pearl studded shirts, black rolled cowboy hats and sporting a few pimples on their lean faces. Peter La Farge put dimes in the juke box and called me over to listen to a brand new song he was excited about. "Heartbreak Hotel." I thought I would never have a bad day.

SUE WEST

Sue West grew up on a ranch outside Santa F. In college she studied creative writing and began teaching ballet in Wyoming in 1970 while raising her three children. She has been artistic director of two dance companies and has received three NEA grants. Voice of America named her an outstanding artist of Montana for her ballet, The Dry Spell, *which won numerous awards. She is founder and producer of Synergy Videos, an exercise video line. She lives near Las Vegas, New Mexico.*

BEFORE SANTA FE BARS

The home on the ranch where I spent my childhood was *adobe*, made of mud bricks by Mexicans a hundred years before my youth. Imperfectly shaped to the closeness of the brown sod and with each room built without forethought to go up and down with the shape of the land. The front porch that held the imperfect, thick walls was supported by white pillars of carved wood, chipped by years of dry winds and blowing New Mexico rains. I adored this home. It had a soul that made each of the children raised under its roof reach out for color and drama in their lives. I was born there in December 1946, the youngest of a family of six, freckled faced, near sighted and slightly redheaded.

"Chaquaco" was our name for this home where I spent my first twenty years. The memories of this time were seldom slow and quiet but exciting and hectic, for the West family had a certain zest for living, a capacity to make each occasion special, stretching it even beyond its due importance. There is not one childhood memory more clear in my heart than the memories of country dances held in the large living room of Chaquaco. I can hear the music and laughter, the whooping and chatter. It wasn't just the dances themselves that I loved but the planning for weeks, and the thrill of the first headlights coming down the hill to reflect off the top of the windmill, followed by the headlights of a long line of cars coming to our dances.

My Irish mother fussed thoroughly about these dances, spending days waxing the brick floors on her knees with her head wrapped in a red bandana, washing windows and baking pies. My daddy on the other hand was easy going, putting off till the last minute the evening milking, and cleaning his boots with his pocket-knife in the kitchen as the first guests would arrive, smiling with easy charm while Mother cleaned up the mess. The dances were the center stage of Daddy's life, the fiddle player his director and each fat or skinny, pretty or homely woman his adoring fan.

The neighbors would come from miles away, the wife with starched petticoats and special cake; and the man, freshly shaven, smelling like the whiskey bottle tucked under his arm. The children came too, very much a part of these nights, running loud and boisterous in and out of the Virginia Reel, playing hide and seek through the rambling dark adobe rooms. We giggled, dancing with timid boys—step one two, one two. Weren't we good at it too? For days before we practiced dancing around the brick floor, often the palm of our own hand the imaginary cheek of our boyfriend. We would eventually fall asleep on a pile of coats to be awakened at dawn when the party ended and the morning milking needed doing.

Perhaps it is the fact those days and times are gone forever that make those nights so important to cherish. My children are making their own memories now, but those type of country people with their complete openness, coming from so far away as families to dance, drink, and visit, no longer seem to exist.

I have a sketch of a country dance hanging in my new home and this sketch is titled "Before Santa Fe Bars." The children in this picture are laughing, weaving in and out of dancing couples, the women poke their heads out of the kitchen, gossiping, a fat lady dances with a tall man and a baby sits on a daddy's shoulder while he taps his foot to the music. This picture is a part of my childhood, my past. Those people came to Chaquaco with rustling skirts and Stetson hats. The faces now become clear in my mind as I see each one. I can even feel Daddy lifting me to his shoulder to dance high above the floor, twirling fast to the quick beat of the fiddle.

JUDY GOLDBERG

Judy Goldberg is an independent radio producer and host of Back Roads Radio. As an educator, Judy has initiated educational programs within the public schools, colleges and museums in community research, communication arts, video and radio production. Judy teaches Narrative Radio and Radio Drama as an adjunct faculty of Santa Fe Community College's Media Arts Department. She also directs the Santa Fe Youth Radio Project.

THROUGH THE LENS

After attending the Anthropology Film Center in Santa Fe, Jeff, a wild-eyed, hard-driving thirty-something hired me for a one-day shoot as an assistant in the production of a thirty second TV spot about senior citizens having to choose between heat and food. Government assistance for the elderly was threatened and images of an empty refrigerator with a pack of bologna and an old man with a crocheted blanket over his shoulders were to deliver the message of need and response. After a successful day's work I was asked if I wanted a job in Las Trampas, a village in the mountains of northern New Mexico and my life took a dramatic and lasting turn.

It was spring 1979 and I was hired to make documentary videos about traditional life, self-reliance and community survival. I worked with three other fellows—Jeff, the fast-brained hippie from Los Angeles; Juan, a Las Trampas native; and Chris, a young, bright, yet floundering, guy from New Jersey.

Jeff spearheaded the Self Reliance Foundation with the explicit purpose of developing a TV series on traditional ways of life, coupled with modern appropriate technology, like solar food dryers and passive solar homes. As a Beverly Hills export, Jeff had lived in Las Trampas since the late sixties. He had been attracted to New Mexico by national news about Reyes Tijerina and the Courthouse Raid in Tierra Amarilla.

"It was a time when locals still took the law into their own hands," he would say, "proving the West was still alive." This single event attracted Jeff to New Mexico. Along with other urban youth of the sixties, Jeff found his way to the isolated communes and eventually to Las Trampas. He bought land and built an adobe home with the help of Juan's father, Tranquilino Lopez, and other villagers. Having come from fast-paced, over-populated Los Angeles, Jeff wanted—as we all did—to communicate how time-honored customs, sweat equity, and neighbors-helping-neighbors could be a model, if not a movement, for revitalizing villages and urban centers, alike.

Each of us had seen how the degradation of small town, rural life was on the rise.

Just like everywhere else in the country, the younger people in northern New Mexico villages were abandoning their towns. Jobs, education, opportunity, and money had lured away those who left. Change for the villages had been taking place for some time, but in the late seventies and early eighties there were still remnants of the old ways and we were heart bent on capturing the images, the observations from the *ancianos* and the wisdom inherent in lives of hard work, devotion and real to goodness, living and breathing, family values.

My days at the foundation were filled with researching and writing grants, writing scripts, shooting and logging footage and editing shows. I need to admit I had mixed feelings in me about our work.

The Lopez family seemed supportive of our efforts to pre-
serve culture and perpetuate a way of life that was dying, but
others perceived us as exploiters—assuming that if we had cameras and recorders we were from Hollywood, therefore making a
lot of money. My short-term CETA position of $5.50 an hour was
something, but making a killing—I don't think so. Yet, the act of
capturing images and sound bites put us on the outside of the real
work. So, as much as possible, I would jump in and do the real
work—turning the soil, irrigating crops, harvesting fruit, shuck-
ing corn, making tortillas, peeling roasted chilies, mixing mud
for plastering the church, chopping wood, feeding chickens and
the like. To be solely the observer, the image gatherer, felt empty.
I, too, wanted to contribute to the necessary work.

The opportunity arrived when I could merge desire to help
and document this way of life. We stood in the fields taping a
horse drawn plow turned the earth. We documented the whole
process of making *chicos*, a traditional way of preserving corn.
We taped Tranquilino as his eighty-year-old cracked and bent
thumb punctured the white kernels of corn on the stalk. If milk
spurted from the broken kernel casing, the corn was ready for
picking. Repositioning the camera we panned as Tranquilino; his
wife, Filia; his daughter, Priscilla; and his nephew, Timmy filled
the sacks and lugged them from the *milpa* to the bank of the acequia
beside the *horno*. In somewhat frantic, yet well-practiced rhythm,
the team of hands wet down the corn, scooping buckets of water
from the *acequia*. Juan scraped out the last shards of hot coals
from the horno before the one-take-only action began. In rapid
fire the green-sheathed cornhusks were whirled into the horno
and the wooden door was securely sealed into place with wet
mud slapped around the edges of the door. Priscilla inserted the
designated rock into the smoke hole and the horno was set to do
its job. Overnight the corn steamed and cooked.

In the brisk early morning light, with the majestic Sangre de
Cristo peaks in the distance, we set up the camera to capture
Tranquilino, hoe in hand, as he pried the mud encased door off of
the horno. As he peeled back the horno's mudded door, we were

engulfed with the wood-smoked aroma of fresh baked corn. One by one the oven-baked cornhusks were peeled back and tossed to the side, until only a few leaves were attached to the cob. The leaves were braided into *ristras* with five or six exposed ears dangling like jewels. The chains of ristras hung on the wire fence to dry. Every once and a while we would snag a fresh ear and chomp down on the steamy, moist, and buttery kernels.

Having the opportunity to live in Las Trampas, to get to know my neighbors, to help them in small ways and to document a life that has all but slipped away was personally invaluable. Nearly thirty years later, I'm still championing the voices and stories of those of humble means and remarkable and bountiful spirit.

TONY PADILLA

Tony Padilla's first language was Spanish. He did not begin to learn English until first grade. Tony has his Master's Degree in English and is a retired high school English teacher who passes his days reading, biking, skiing, fishing, and shooting pool. He is also an excellent native New Mexican cook.

COPING WITH CHANGE

I had just finished reading Alvin Toffler's *Future Shock* at the end of a somewhat difficult school term, and it fittingly related to what was happening in my life. For years I had felt that I was losing grips on my culture. Santa Fe, which I had always considered my refuge, was also changing at an alarming rate.

I've always understood that change is inevitable. It was the rapid, out of control change that was beginning to make me feel nervous and uncomfortable. I found myself resisting with feeble lines of defense. I attempted to maintain cultural ties by indulging in the time-honored tradition of cutting and gathering wood in autumn with Bill Lucero, a long-time friend. We are both old and the wood cutting gets more difficult with each passing year, but we refuse to quit this fall ritual, no matter how much it hurts. We seem to inspire each other and we are tenaciously hanging on to this cultural tradition. This fall ritual has helped keep cultural ties intact. To this day, my sole source of home heating is my wood stove. There is nothing that generates heat like burning wood. Cooking is yet another means by which I attempt to hold on to my culture. I continue to follow the "Do it by feel" recipes of four generations of my family. Maintaining contact with the Spanish-speaking populace has also been very comforting.

On a broader level, societal change has been occurring at a tremendous pace. Santa Fe, which had always been a sort of security blanket for me, has now taken on new and ugly hues. This, coupled with mind-spinning changes in technology, has made me even more anxious. I tried to keep these changes at arm's length by refusing to use or own many modern devices. I seldom answer the phone. I don't own a cell phone. I'm not wired to the Internet since I don't own a computer, and I prefer writing with a pencil rather than working with a word processor. I also prefer a bicycle to a car. Some people may shake their heads at these inconsequential acts of defiance, but they work for me.

At any rate, what I had read in *Future Shock* prompted me into taking more control of my life and slowing it down in the process. Since the school term was almost over, and as a high school teacher facing almost three months of free time, I began to consider different things I could do to help me maintain a proper balance and perspective in my life.

Like Thoreau when he went to Walden Pond, I wanted to slow down and really look at people and things that were around me. In essence, I wanted to live deliberately, and I wanted to reduce life to its simplest denominator.

After some thought on the subject, it occurred to me that a trip through rural America would be my Walden Pond. The emphasis would be on the journey rather than the destination. I would turn it into the discovery of a quieter and simpler America. The mode of transportation I chose was the bicycle. The very act of turning bicycle cranks is deliberate and simple, so the bicycle also served as a symbol of how I wanted to live that summer.

In early June I loaded panniers along with a small tent and a sleeping bag, secured them to two bicycle racks, and off I went into the unknown. What I found was an amazing diversity of ideas and moods. I saw kindness and intolerance, frustration and hope, anger and cheer, poverty and wealth, and ignorance and intelligence.

I began the ride in Albuquerque and I headed west on Interstate 40. I rode through half of New Mexico and half of Arizona. Arriving in Los Angeles I found a saloon near the beach. The bar displayed a large open window with a heavy wooden shutter and I figured I could leave my bike on the bar wall and still be able to keep a close watch over it.

I walked into the semi-dark bar wearing spandex shorts. The floor was layered with about an inch of sawdust. I saw a couple of shabby pool tables and a bar that I thought was too low, which was made of a very rough, splintered wood. I worked my way over to an empty bar stool and ordered a beer. As my eyes adjusted to the dim light inside, I saw a Hell's Angel logo on a black jacket. Then I saw another and another.

Unwittingly, I had stumbled into a Hell's Angel's hangout. Several members of the group stared at my spandex shorts and then at my bicycle, which was leaning in full view against the window. The tension was so intense that it seemed to strain the rustic wooden walls that held the place intact. Finally, one angel connecting me with the bike broke the silence and asked me where I was coming from. I told him that I had ridden from Santa Fe. At that point, quiet fell over the bar, and I could again feel more stares. One guy finally broke the silence. He laughed, then bellowed, "You got some balls." The whole bar echoed in laughter.

I drank more than I intended that afternoon. I never paid for a drink and I learned that under a very tough veneer, these Angels were really sensitive, caring, and generous people.

I settled down on the warm sands of Hermosa Beach that evening. The setting sun, followed by the rolling fog, was so spectacular that it will be forever etched on my mind. The lapping waves and the swooshing ocean lulled me into a deep sleep.

Twenty-one days and fourteen hundred miles after leaving Santa Fe I arrived at my destination where I dipped my front wheel in the cold waters of the San Francisco Bay.

This was not the end of the journey. The seed to discover, to know, and to understand had been planted.

The following summer I flew to Portland, Oregon with bike in tow. I rode the back roads of Oregon into Idaho, Montana, Wyoming, Colorado, and finally New Mexico, attempting to connect with this land and the simplicity of its rural people.

The next summer I pointed Rosinante II eastward and headed towards the waters of the Atlantic.

Riding through Kansas on an especially blustery day, I arrived in Eureka after eighty-some miles of fighting strong headwinds. I immediately went in search of the local pub, as had become my custom at the end of a day's ride. I found the only cafe and bar in town, and ordered a beer. I sat in a half trance, sipping my beer and reminiscing over the day's ride. I snapped back to reality as a large plate cradling an equally large steak was placed before me. I stammered and then quickly informed the waitress that I hadn't placed an order. She smiled and then pointed to a couple sitting across the cafe and said, "Their treat."

I walked over to their table and thanked them. They told me that they had passed me thirty-five miles from town and that they thought that a steak dinner was an appropriate meal for someone who had been riding in such a fierce headwind. They commended me on my courage and sense of adventure and wished out loud that they could try something like that.

After a pleasant conversation and a good dinner, I walked my bike across the street and set up camp in Eureka's city park. I was content and slept well that night. I was at peace with the world. In the morning I broke camp, loaded my bicycle, and walked across the street for breakfast. I ordered pancakes, and as I ate, an old lady walked over to my table and let me know that the whole neighborhood had looked over me as I slept. She touched my hand and gave me her blessings for a good journey. I left Eureka with a good feeling about people and the way things were.

Toffler's *Future Shock* was but a faded remembrance.

The feelings of peace and harmony were marred when I arrived at Yates Corner, Kansas. I stopped for a coke at a general store when I was approached by a man who was driving a sixteen-wheeler across the state. He gruffly let me know that I had no business riding a bike on a highway. He told me that if he saw me on the highway on his return trip that he would run me down and kill me.

In a small town in Missouri, a jewelry maker who was dying of lung cancer invited me to his modest home for a simple spaghetti dinner. After dinner he proudly showed me some of his creations while his wife readied the kids for bed. Quiet fell on the household, and we retreated to a swing hanging on a porch that was in desperate need of paint. We sat in the languid and humid Missouri night and talked about change and unfulfilled dreams till very late. That night I slept on their weathered couch, which smelled of wet dog. I didn't mind though; because of the kindness and generosity shown me, I slept contentedly. To this day I can see the haunting eyes of the jewelry maker's wife. She knew that her life would soon change, and the hurt and sorrow in her eyes was undeniable. The artist must be dead by now, and I often wonder how she and her now grown kids have adapted to this most horrible change.

Two days' ride into Kentucky I took a wrong turn and ended up pushing my bike through heavy brush and down a road that had deteriorated to something that resembled a cow path. I worked my way to a clearing and spotted what seemed to be a cabin in the distance. I veered the bicycle in that direction. As I approached what I could now discern was a rustic cabin, I could see a man, feet apart, with long scraggly red hair and a beard of the same color. He held a rifle in the crook of his arm. I greeted him and let him know that I was lost. He studied me suspiciously, calculated that I was no threat, and relaxed his grip on the rifle. We talked, and as we did so, I noticed that there were pot plants growing as high as the roof. He invited me for a breakfast of pancakes and grits. I teased and played silly word and face games with his two shy young daughters after breakfast. The man and I then talked

about the economic hardships of rural Kentucky, and we acknowl-
edged that growing pot was a means of survival. We talked most
of the morning, then we placed my bike in the back of his rusted
pickup, and he drove me to the road I had missed earlier.

At the end of another day's ride in Kentucky I was setting up
camp in a state park. The park ranger drove up, and we talked as
I set up camp. He told me that he had moved from Chicago to
rural Kentucky because he wanted to get away from crime-in-
fested Chicago. He then paused, and sadly revealed that Chicago
does not hold a monopoly on crime and violence. He had found it
in Kentucky also, and that stark realization was only too clear in
his voice and in his eyes. The ranger left. About an hour later
what he knew to be true revealed itself.

A car with very drunk and very mean looking young guys
drove up to my campsite. The driver revved the engine, and all
five occupants sat in the car, giving me menacing stares. I could
see beer cans and a bottle covering faces and the threats they
held. For a moment I felt a surge of fear and panic. My equipment
was scattered throughout the campsite and there was really no
place for me to run. I tried to control my fear, but the roaring
engine, the stares, and the chatter in the car only made the panic
worse. The fear was so intense that I could no longer think clearly.
As a last desperate act, I sauntered over to the car and very cock-
ily blurted out, "How about giving me a beer."

This disarmed the group. The silence was deafening as mouths
dropped open, showing uneven yellow-stained teeth. I especially
remember the shocked disbelief in those eyes that earlier had ex-
pressed a threat. Seconds passed. I expected a reaction, and they
realized that they had to react to my brazen request. The driver
opened the car door, and the back door opened at the same time.
Two, and then another, exited the car. The moment of truth. The
driver walked to the trunk, opened it, and pulled a beer out of the
cooler and handed it to me. I had them. I felt in control. I guzzled
the beer in three slugs, burped, bent the can, and asked for another. Mouths fell open again. Almost in disbelief, the driver
opened the cooler and pulled out another beer.

At this point all five were out of the car, and we were talking like long lost friends. At one point, a fellow who was sitting on the picnic table fell to the ground with a loud thud. Two others picked him up and threw him in the back seat. The driver then summoned me to the trunk of the car, unwrapped a blanket, and showed me a shotgun that he claimed he had used to shoot and kill a guy who had been making advances on his sister. They ran out of beer shortly thereafter, piled into the car, and assured me that they would return with more beer and moonshine. They drove off, and as the dust began to settle, my tent and belongings were on my bike and a new trail of dust was beginning to form on that dirt road in rural Kentucky where a park ranger had resettled to escape big city crime and violence.

I rode through Virginia with little fanfare or serious incident. I remember that at this point in my travels, modesty was something I had left somewhere 2 thousand miles back. Since I was at all times riding rural roads, there was almost always a stream flowing close by. Out of necessity and without a concern for modesty, I would stop and wash in whichever stream was at hand. Once as I was bathing, a motorist drove by. He stopped, backed the car, and the occupants stared while I sat in the stream naked. I smiled and waved. They nodded and drove off.

The ride culminated on the shores of the Atlantic ocean in Virginia. This odyssey through rural America began as a quest for cultural and community stability. I had traveled the back roads at fifteen miles per hour, covering an average of seventy-five miles per day. At such a pace, I was able to place people and things in proper perspective. I learned that no matter how rapidly things change, I can still maintain cultural integrity by living deliberately and simply. The ride ended, but the people I met and the lessons I learned continue to nurture and comfort me to this day. At times, when I begin to feel overwhelmed by a changing world and a dying culture, I remember Thoreau's sojourn at Walden Pond. He went there to live deliberately and simply, and with that thought in mind, I mount my trusty steed and pedal through scenic New Mexico.

GLOSSARY

acequia, f.s. Irrigation ditch.
Acequia Baranca. Baranca irrigation ditch.
adios. Goodbye.
adobe, m.s. Brick made of mud and straw.
alabados, m.pl. Hymns; praise.
Algunas pobres solamente habian bailado los ojos. Some
    poor souls only danced their eyes.
ancianos, m.pl. Elders.
baile, m.s. Dance.
biscochito, m. s., *biscochitos,* m. pl. Official New Mexico
    state cookie.
Bracero program. Laborers' program.
cabrera, f.s. Goatherd.
calabacitas, f. pl. Squash; zuccini.
carne molida, f. Hamburger, ground meat.
cerco, m.s. Fence.
cerveza, f.s. Beer.
chile, m.s. Spicy seasoning; a stew; a sauce; peppers.
chili verde. Green chili.
chicas, f. pl. Girls.
chicos, m.pl. Dried corn cooked in an oven.
comino, m.s. Cumin.
cuadrilla, f.s.*; cuadrillas,* f. pl. Quadrille; a kind of dance.
cuenta, f.s. Tale, story; bill.
desaigre, m.s. The snub; turn down an inviation to dance.
disciplinas, f. pl. Punishments; whips.
el baile del pano. The handkerchief dance.
empanadas, f. pl. Turnovers; fried fruit or meat pies.
gallina culeca, f.s. Setting hen.
Hay Chihuahua. Ow! wow!

hermanidad, m.s. Brotherhood.

Hermanos de Jesus. Brotherhood of Jesus.

hermanos, m.pl. Brothers.

hito, m.s. , *hita,* f.s. Affectionate term for son, daughter.

hoja, f.s. Leaf.

horno, m.s. Outdoor oven.

Juareñas mojadas, f.pl. Wetbacks from Juarez.

loco, m.s.; *loca,* f.s. Crazy man, crazy woman.

luna, f.s. Moon.

madero, m.s. Cross.

mala, f.s. Mean.

mantanza, f.s.; *matanzas,* f.pl. Butchering.

mayordomo. m.s. Steward; man in charge of the acequia.

mi. My.

mi hita, f.s. My daughter.

milpa, f.s. Large garden; cornfield.

molino, m.s. Mill.

monja, f.s. Nun.

morada, f.s. House, dwelling.

morado, m.s. The color purple.

morodo, m.s. Dummy.

percha, f.s. Clothesline.

pecheras, f.pl. Coveralls.

pilón, m.s. An extra item for free; gratuity.

portal, f.s. Porch.

posole, m. Boiled corn; stew made with boiled corn, meat
  and chile pods.

quelites, m. Spinach.

rezador, m.s. Prayer leader.

ristra, f.s. String of chiles.

rueditas, f.pl. Dried circles of squash.

salsa, f.s. Spicey sauce.

saltio, m.s. A type of tile used for flooring.

tamale, m.s. Meat filling inside corn mash, wrapped in corn husk.

tarimas, f.pl. Long, heavy wooden benches.

tequila, f. A liquor made from cactus.

tio, m.s., *tia*, f.s. Uncle, aunt.

valse, m.s. Waltz.

vayan con Dios. Go with God; goodbye.

vecina, f.s.; *vecino*, m.s. Neighbor (lady); neighbor (man).

velorios, m.pl. Wakes.

viga, f.s. Rafter.

visitas, f.pl. Visits.

viva: Hurray; long live _____ (as in *Viva Mexico!*)

vuelvan pronto. Come back soon.

y. And.